What a great, fun book! Larry Osborne's *A Contrarian's Guide* made me cringe at certain intersections; at other times I felt the thrill of someone putting into words what I've always felt. He takes the cookies off the top shelf and puts them where we all can enjoy them, as he finishes our incomplete sentences and makes us feel like geniuses.

It's a quick read that's filled with brilliant, disturbing insights. He may not change stodgy theologians, but he may just annoy them closer to Jesus.

WAYNE CORDEIRO
Coauthor of *Culture Shift*
Senior Pastor, New Hope Christian Fellowship
O'ahu Honolulu

Larry Osborne hits it out of the park with *A Contrarian's Guide to Knowing God*. Practical and engaging, this book calls each of us to a new way of thinking about what it means to build a great relationship with God.

It does what every great book has always done: It causes some of us relief, it causes some of us great consternation, and it causes all of us to stop and think about what we're doing and why we're doing it.

The concepts Larry shares have blessed and encouraged me as a follower of Christ and a leader in His church. I will definitely move this book to the top of my must-read list for our church family.

TOBY SLOUGH
Author of *Living the Dream* and *The Great Adventure*
Senior Pastor, Cross Timbers Community Church
Argyle, Texas

This is a refreshingly helpful book for everyone who loves Jesus but has struggled with tidy formulas for spiritual growth.

MARK DRISCOLL
Author of *The Radical Reformission*
Cofounder and President, Acts 29 Church Planting Network
Founder, Mars Hill Church
Seattle

Rich wisdom brilliantly communicated by a very talented writer. Takes the blinders off and opens your eyes to some strange and unique ways God works.

STEPHEN ARTERBURN
Author of *The Secrets Men Keep*
Founder and Chairman, New Life Ministries
Radio Cohost of *New Life Live*

This book will speak to everyone who has ever felt "left out" spiritually. Larry's insights cut through the commonly accepted, guilt-induced world of religion as he captures the raw essence of New Testament relationship.

Reading this book feels like a conversation with Jesus over coffee— simple, profound, biblical, yet completely opposite of what I've learned from America's polluted version of Christianity.

Every year, one book grabs my attention and speaks to my soul. *A Contrarian's Guide to Knowing God* is this year's book.

CRAIG GROESCHEL
Author of *Chazown* and *Confessions of a Pastor*
Senior Pastor, LifeChurch.tv
Oklahoma City

Larry Osborne puts into words what many of us have wondered about for years but never had the courage to voice publicly. This book affirms us as individuals with unique personalities, learning styles, and gifts while offering sound counsel on the importance of deepening our relationships with God and with each other.

A Contrarian's Guide to Knowing God gives us permission to trade our feelings of spiritual inferiority for the confidence to pursue a life with God at the very center of who we are and how we choose to live each day.

LINDA STANLEY
Director, Next Generation Pastors Leadership Community Leadership Network

I've heard all my life that God created each of us uniquely. Larry opened my eyes to the truth that God desires us to know and follow Him as an expression of that uniqueness.

With a keen mixture of wit, wisdom, and God's word, *A Contrarian's Guide to Knowing God* provides a refreshing and insightful look at how the "average guy" can enjoy a meaningful, guilt-free relationship with God.

CHIP HENDERSON
Senior Pastor, Pinelake Church
Brandon, Mississippi

As a pastor of a church where the average age is twenty-six, I am always looking for down-to-earth resources that will encourage spiritual growth for the "normal people" who come to our church. This book will be at the top of our resource list! Whether you are a seasoned believer or a seeker, *A*

Contrarian's Guide to Knowing God: Spirituality for the Rest of Us will challenge, encourage, and move you to follow Jesus.

DARRIN PATRICK
Founding Pastor, The Journey
St. Louis

Larry Osborne has mapped out a brand-new path for spiritual formation in *A Contrarian's Guide to Knowing God.* This is one of the only books I know that takes you on the path to God without insisting that you be more disciplined and more structured, and that you read a lot more.

Finally, a book for the rest of us!

DAVE FERGUSON
Coauthor of *The Big Idea*
Lead Pastor and Spiritual Entrepreneur
Community Christian Church and NewThing Network
Chicago

If you've ever thought you were the only one challenging a cookie-cutter approach to faith, you need to read this book. Thank God! Osborne shows us how our relationship with God is not a one-size-fits-all approach.

BILL EASUM
Easum-Bandy Associates
Coauthor of *Go Big* and *Beyond the Box*

Larry Osborne has always seen things a little differently. His fresh look at the church has led to a multisite revolution; now Larry gives us a fresh look at spiritual life that is just as helpful and thought provoking. I highly recommend it.

ROBERT LEWIS
Coauthor of *Culture Shift* and *The Church of Irresistible Influence*
Founder, Men's Fraternity
Pastor-at-large, Fellowship Bible Church
Little Rock

Larry challenges current notions of spiritual development in a healthy and thoughtful way. Whether you are beginning your journey with God or have been at it a long time, this book will be a powerful blessing and guide.

BOB ROBERTS JR.
Founder of Glocalnet
Senior Pastor, NorthWood Church
Fort Worth, Texas

I've known Larry for years, and he always mentors me personally with his insights into following Jesus. For the first time, he's captured those simple lessons in this great book.

A Contrarians Guide to Knowing God brings fresh insights from the Bible to help us conquer the nagging fears and doubts we have about our walk with Christ. This confident work, clearly illustrated by Scripture and life stories, helps leaders and believers realize that the key essentials in a growing relationship are not what we think.

DAVE TRAVIS
Coauthor of *Beyond the Box*
Executive Vice President, Leadership Network

Finally! In the midst of all the left-brained spiritual growth strategies available, Larry has written a guide for the rest of us. If your soul is yearning for practical, real-time help that works on Monday as well as Sunday, this book is for you.

JIM DENISON
Pastor of Teaching, Park Cities Baptist Church
Dallas

I read the book in one sitting. It is engaging, convicting, maddening, and encouraging. I hope it is widely read to correct spiritual abuses and encourage the majority of everyday Christians (whom Osborne calls "cobblers in Corinth").

When I finished *A Contrarian's Guide,* I felt free and relieved. Osborne took off weight after weight of spiritual "churchy" expectations for someone who sincerely wants to be godly. I felt like singing, "Trust and obey, for there's no other way…"

Larry's *A Contrarian's Guide* opened my eyes to ways I have distorted the simple New Testament picture of godliness because of my zeal to motivate. My congregation should thank Larry for saving them from *me*.

BRUCE MILLER
Coauthor of *The Leadership Baton*
Senior Pastor, McKinney Fellowship Bible Church
McKinney, Texas

A CONTRARIAN'S

GUIDE TO KNOWING GOD

LARRY
OSBORNE

Multnomah Books

A CONTRARIAN'S GUIDE TO KNOWING GOD
published by Multnomah Books

© 2007 by Larry Osborne
International Standard Book Number: 978-1-59052-794-8

Cover design by DesignWorks Group, Inc.
Cover image by Getty Images
Interior design and typeset by Pamela McGrew

Italics in Scripture quotations are the author's emphasis.
Scripture quotations are from:
The Holy Bible, New International Version
© 1973, 1984 by International Bible Society,
used by permission of Zondervan Publishing House

Published in the United States by WaterBrook Multnomah, an imprint of the
Crown Publishing Group, a division of Random House Inc., New York.

MULTNOMAH and its mountain colophon are registered trademarks of Random
House Inc.

Printed in the United States of America
ALL RIGHTS RESERVED
No part of this publication may be reproduced, stored in a retrieval system,
or transmitted, in any form or by any means—electronic, mechanical,
photocopying, recording, or otherwise—without prior written permission.

For information:
MULTNOMAH BOOKS
12265 Oracle Boulevard, Suite 200
Colorado Springs, Colorado 80921

Library of Congress Cataloging-in-Publication Data
Osborne, Larry W., 1952-
  A contrarian's guide to knowing God : spirituality for the rest of
us / by Larry Osborne.
    p. cm.
  ISBN 1-59052-794-1
  1. Spirituality. 2. God (Christianity)—Knowableness. I. Title.
BV4501.3.O83 2007
248—dc22

                                   2006036716

10 11 12—10 9 8 7 6 5 4

To Jesus my Savior, the one who knows me most
intimately and still likes me anyway.
My hope is that I've helped a few people to
know you better and please you more.

To Nancy, Nathan, Rachel and Joshua,
thank you for the love and joy you bring my way.
You've been the greatest gifts of my life.

CONTENTS

INTRODUCTION: A DIFFERENT PATH 15
THE PURPOSES AND GOALS OF THIS BOOK... *Why
the New Testament was written in the street language of the
marketplace... How our zeal to honor God can mess up
everything... Why we keep raising the bar—and why it needs to
be lowered...*

PART ONE
GENUINE SPIRITUALITY

1. SPIRITUALITY FOR THE REST OF US 21
WHAT DOES IT MEAN TO KNOW GOD?... *Why do
most of the books on spirituality and the inner life make us feel
so inadequate?... Does God prefer smart people who read
well?... What little children teach us about Bible scholars? And
what exactly does contrarian mean?...*

2. RELIGION OR RELATIONSHIP? 27
THE DIFFERENCE BETWEEN RELIGION AND
RELATIONSHIP... *The tell-tale marks of religion... The one
and only thing all relationships have in common... What Matt's
second wife taught me about God... How an old hippie, a cop,
and their father reveal the essence of a great relationship with
God...*

3. JESUS OR JOHN? 35
HOW TWO UTTERLY DIFFERENT PEOPLE CAN
BOTH PLEASE GOD... *The problem with the Blank Slate
Theory, and why the kids prefer Disneyland... Why John had his
doubts about Jesus?... Why Jesus had no doubts about John...
The one thing that matters most...*

4. IS IT A SIN TO BE AVERAGE? 43
WHY LEADERSHIP SHOULD NEVER BE CONFUSED
WITH SPIRITUALITY... *Why most churches and most
pastors treat low-drive Christians as losers... Why it's okay to be
spiritually average—or below average... The cobbler in
Corinth?... The problem with drive-by guiltings?... The ultimate
goal of spirituality...*

PART TWO

HOW DOES SPIRITUAL GROWTH HAPPEN?

5. THE CASE FOR MEANDERING 53
THE WAY MOST PEOPLE GROW... *Why linear and
sequential discipleship programs so often miss the boat... How
the need to grow and the need to know accelerate spiritual
growth... How most people learn—what we remember and
why... The stickiness factor...*

6. VELCROED FOR GROWTH. 61
HOW SMALL GROUPS CHANGE EVERYTHING...
*Why the primary reason to be in a small group is not what most
people think it is... Velcroed for growth: What does that mean
and how does it work?... The upside of peer pressure?... Three
reasons why small groups make everyone more honest...*

7. THE DIMMER SWITCH PRINCIPLE. 71
WHY IT'S SO ESSENTIAL TO OBEY THE LIGHT WE
HAVE... *The Three Strike Rule... What happens when God
becomes a cosmic consultant... The Dimmer Switch Principle...
How I almost stepped on a bear, and what it taught me about
spiritual enlightenment... Why the amount of light we have isn't
nearly as important as what we do with it...*

8. INSIDE OUT 79
HOW THE HOLY SPIRIT DOES EXACTLY WHAT
JESUS SAID HE WOULD DO... *What the disciples didn't
understand the first time... Why it's a good thing Jesus isn't here
anymore... From "with us" to "in us," and why that's so
important... Static on the line—and how to get rid of it... The
Prayer of Permission...*

PART THREE
WHAT DOES GOD WANT?

9. THE HIGH PLACE PRINCIPLE
Blind Spots—Yours, Mine, and Theirs. 93
WHY GOD SO OFTEN BLESSES AND USES THE
WRONG PEOPLE... *What a chronic deceiver, a horn-dog
judge, and a never-believe-God-the-first-time warrior had in
common... Why your blinds spots don't look like a blind spots to
me, and why I think my blind spots are no big deal... Solomon's
big day, and why God shouldn't have shown up—but showed up
anyway...*

10. THE MUSTARD SEED PRINCIPLE
Is Faith Overrated? 103
WHY YOU PROBABLY DON'T NEED MORE FAITH...
*Can faith and doubt coexist?... Is knowledge a detriment to
faith?... Why most of our definitions of faith have nothing to do
with how the Bible defines it... Two examples of pretty lame
faith... Mustard seeds... What getting on an airplane can teach
us about faith and God...*

11. WHAT'S ZEAL GOT TO DO WITH IT?
First Love Lost 115
WHY SPIRITUAL ZEAL ISN'T NEARLY AS
IMPORTANT AS WE'VE BEEN LED TO BELIEVE...
Why intensity doesn't last, and why that's not a bad thing... The

church that lost that lovin' feeling... The truth about David's passion and zeal... Two words that most English-speaking Christians tend to misunderstand... The kind of love God wants to see...

12. FENCES

Helping God Out? 125
WHY EXTRA RULES AND REGULATIONS UNDERCUT GENUINE SPIRITUALITY... *Gold-package Christians and the three things they usually share in common... Helping God out—and why the Apostle Paul thought it was such a bad idea... How a blustering parent's empty threats are a lot like our extra rules... A story about electric fences... A rushed baptism... Didn't God get it right the first time?...*

13. BEST PRACTICES OVERLOAD

Comparison's Curse 135
WHY TOO MANY SPIRITUAL HEROES CAN MESS YOU UP... *What happens when we try to incorporate all the best traits of all the best Christians?... A stroll down Madison Avenue... How Mother Teresa gave me a nervous twitch... What Michael Jordon's struggle to hit a curve ball can teach us about God's gifts and calling... Why it's no big deal if our eyes don't hear too well...*

14. GIFT PROJECTION

Chocolate-Covered Arrogance 143
WHY PROJECTING OUR CALLING ONTO EVERYONE ELSE TICKS GOD OFF... *Why we see some needs so clearly... Why others blow right past us... How did a struggle with spiritual pride ever become a badge of honor?... Why missionaries, evangelists, and Bible teachers are the worst gift projectors... Why those with gifts of helps, mercy and administration seldom make us feel guilty... The one thing you should never feel inadequate about...*

15. SEEKING BALANCE

Does God Give a Rip? 151
WHY THE QUEST FOR BALANCE IS A GOOFY
IDEA... *A friend's surprising suggestion... Wasn't Moses a little
out of whack?... What about David, Jeremiah, Peter, Paul?...
What if you're about to fall over?... Three important
questions... The one thing God won't ask us when we stand
before him—and the one thing he will...*

16. WHY RESULTS DON'T MATTER

Inner Peace, Success, and Failure 159
WHY INNER PEACE, SUCCESS, AND FAILURE CAN'T
BE TRUSTED... *Why prisons are full of people who followed
their conscience... What Job's run of bad luck and Samson's run
of good luck reveal about the true meaning of results... Uzziah's
terrible miscalculation... Failure's biggest lie... Do valleys always
mean a wrong turn?...*

17. PREPARING THE HORSE

Lessons from the Unseen Realm 169
IF WE CAN'T CONTROL OUTCOMES, WHAT
SHOULD WE FOCUS ON?... *My three Dark Years and
what they taught me about pride... The one thing no one can
control; the one thing everyone can control... The unseen realm
and Joshua's peek behind the curtain...*

18. TOOLS OR RULES?

Finding What Works for You 177
WHY TOOLS FOR GROWTH SHOULD NEVER BE
TURNED INTO RULES FOR GROWTH... *The key
difference between a tool and a rule... How tools become rules...
What happens when we confuse descriptions with
prescriptions?... Why your church might not want to be a New
Testament church after all... Why the right tool for me is
probably the wrong tool for you...*

19. THE POTENTIAL TRAP

Why Being All We Can Be Might Be a Dumb Idea. 187
THE TRUTH ABOUT UNFULFILLED POTENTIAL...
*How a great commercial ended up giving terrible advice... Why
the Parable of the Talents isn't really about our talents... The
compass called potential; where and what it usually points to...
Why happy talk stinks... Why I stopped writing and why I'm
back at it... A touching love story...*

20. GLASS HOUSE LIVING

Why Accountability Groups Don't Work 199
THE BEST TOOL FOR STAYING ON THE STRAIGHT
AND NARROW... *Why accountability groups are overrated...
The one thing they do well... Why they're not very good at
preventing sin... The truth about shame... Our culture's love
affair with the right to privacy... The power of clear windows and
an open door... Why everyone lives better when mom's watching...*

21. PRIORITY NUMBER ONE?

Why Putting God First Might Be a Bad Idea 209
PUTTING GOD WHERE HE BELONGS... *What does it
mean to "put God first"? Why it's a bad idea... "In Jesus name"—
it's way more than the "send" button for prayer... How God got
stuffed into a box... Why the enemy loves the spiritual/secular
dichotomy... The truth about full-time Christian ministry...*

EPILOGUE: A FINAL WORD

Keeping It Simple. 217
WHAT I HOPE YOU'VE GOTTEN FROM THIS
BOOK... *How Christianity is a lot like a regulated
profession... What most non-Christians don't know, and most
Christians no longer seem to believe... Micah's simple advice...*

ACKNOWLEDGMENTS 221

NOTES 223

A DIFFERENT PATH

IT'S NO ACCIDENT that Jesus was raised in a backwater town and used simple illustrations to convey profound truth.

It's no accident the New Testament was written in the simple language of the marketplace rather than classical Greek—which was far more eloquent but way beyond the grasp of the common man.

It was all part of God's plan to make the inaccessible accessible.

When Jesus burst onto the stage, he confronted a religious system that saw God as anything but accessible. Spirituality was reserved for the elite—those with pedigree, education, and a commitment to rigid self-discipline.

He countered this with a different path, one that farmers, fishermen, carpenters, even little children and sinners could follow.

He raised the bar of righteousness. But he lowered the bar to entry.

THIS BOOK AIMS to follow in his footsteps. It's designed to challenge many of our modern-day, widely accepted, and deeply entrenched ideas about what it means to know God, and about what it is that actually produces spirituality. Because too often, in our own zeal to honor God, we've re-raised the bar with definitions of spirituality that are once again beyond the reach of the common man—and more importantly, beyond the heights set by God himself.

While genuine spirituality at its core is quite simple (obey God and follow the unique path he's designed for each of us), it can be extraordinarily complex in its outworking and its many facets. We'll explore those facets as if examining a diamond, closely inspecting and pointing out the beauty and flaws in each one.

IN THE FIRST SECTION we'll attempt to define spirituality—what it is and what it isn't. In the next, we'll explore what it takes to get there from here. And in the final section, we'll examine in depth what God wants and expects from each of us as individuals.

While you'll find many of my observations to be contrarian, I've attempted to carefully run everything through a biblical grid. I encourage you to test it in that light. Hold on to what fits, cast out the rest.

WHAT'S HERE FOR YOU

I've written with three kinds of readers in mind.

First, many of us have tried the standard recipes for knowing God but found them wanting. If that's you, this book is designed to offer hope—and some practical paths to get there.

Second, many of us have learned to play the church game well but we're haunted by nagging doubts—especially about whether everything really works as advertised. I've tried to ask those tough questions and perhaps give a few surprising answers along the way.

Finally, you may have mastered the standard disciplines of spirituality and found them to be incredibly helpful. This book will help you understand the rest of us.

These pages aren't meant to denigrate or devalue the spiritual disciplines. It's not meant to downgrade the help they've given so many. It's simply meant to offer insight into the minds and hearts of those who don't read so well, who work with their hands instead of their minds, who still show a few symptoms of ADD, or who view three days of reflective solitude in a monastery as worse than hell itself.

I think you'll discover that such people aren't necessarily lazy, spiritually dull, or uninterested after all. Often they're just wired differently. And that means their path to spirituality and knowing God will look a lot different from the well-trod and well-signed routes.

Blessings on the journey,
Larry Osborne

1

GENUINE SPIRITUALITY

CHAPTER ONE

SPIRITUALITY FOR THE
REST OF US

I'VE NOTICED that much (if not most) teaching on spirituality is a lot like books I've read on marriage.

My wife and I always thought we had a great one until we started reading books and going to the conferences designed to tell us how to have a great marriage.

We viewed our relationship as characterized by oneness of spirit, soul, and mind—a connectedness that made two truly become one. But the books and conferences informed us that we were doing it all wrong. We weren't eating enough meals together, the TV was on too much, our date nights were far too rare, and our prayer time as a couple was sorely lacking.

The message was clear: The fact that we had a strong marriage didn't matter; how we got there was what mattered most. And we'd apparently gotten there the wrong way.

Their *tools* for building a great marriage had somehow become the *measure* of a great marriage.

And on that scale, we didn't measure up.

COOKIE-CUTTER CHRISTIANS

When it comes to having a great relationship with God, the same thing often happens. The tools and spiritual disciplines that can help us get there frequently become an end in themselves. Books and conferences on the inner life end up presenting a cookie-cutter approach to spirituality that focuses more on the steps we take than on the actual quality of our walk with God.

The emphasis of this book is that God wants a great relationship with all of us, but it can't be found in a one-size-fits-all approach.

It's the end result that matters, not the path we take to get there. If something produces a great walk with God for you, it's a great path to take. If not, it's probably a waste of time, even if lots of other folks highly recommend it.

Fact is, what works for one can be worthless—even harmful—for another. The way we're wired really matters. Whenever we project what works for us onto everyone else, we create frustration and legalism. When we let others project their stuff onto us we too often end up with unfounded guilt or a nervous twitch. Neither of which is very helpful when it comes to producing a great relationship with God.

DOES GOD PLAY FAVORITES?

As a new Christian, the more I pursued what it meant to know God and experience genuine spirituality, the more I found many of the standard answers confusing.

The conventional paths to pleasing God seemed heavily tilted in the direction of certain personality types. The playing field didn't appear to be level. I wondered if God played favorites.

On the one hand, I was told that spirituality was within the reach of everyone. On the other hand, I noticed that almost all the books on spirituality and the inner life were written by introverts—smart ones at that.

I got the distinct impression that God was somehow partial to reflective types with high IQs, impressive vocabularies, and lots of self-discipline. And that left a lot of us on the outside looking in.

> Almost all the books on spirituality and the inner life are written by introverts—smart ones at that.

DO GOOD READERS MAKE BETTER CHRISTIANS?

I also noticed that reading seemed to be rather important. I'm obviously not down on reading, or why write a book? But I'm not quite sure how the ability to read well became the essential tool for spiritual growth.

If I want to know God and experience genuine spirituality, I'm told to read the Bible daily. If I want to grow *really* deep, I'm told to also read the time-honored classics written by the saints of old.

Now, I know the Bible is important; no argument there. But if daily Bible reading and mining the depths of the ancient scholars and mystics is the key to knowing God and God-pleasing spirituality, I wonder how regular folks got there before Gutenberg invented his printing press?

Even more to the point, if reading skills are so vital, how can my friend Tony, who's severely dyslexic, ever hope to know God?

DO BIBLE SCHOLARS MAKE BETTER CHRISTIANS?

I was also puzzled by our widespread emphasis on proper doctrine as central to having a good relationship with God.

I want to make it clear that I personally believe theology and sound doctrine are important—incredibly important. What I believe about God has an undeniable impact on how I live. Wrong thinking leads to wrong decisions; always has, always will.

But didn't Jesus say something about the kingdom of heaven belonging to those who are like little children? If he really meant it, how does our insistence on sound doctrine being essential for knowing and pleasing God fit in with a child's theological naiveté?

Anyone who has ever been around a children's Sunday school class knows that these kids have some pretty messed-up theology. They haven't got a clue about propitiation, the Trinity, or any of the other important doctrines of Scripture. If asked, they'll say the darnedest things.

But as Jesus pointed out, many of them can and do have a great relationship with God—and often, a relationship worth emulating.

That's caused me to wonder if sound doctrine is perhaps more the *result* of knowing and pleasing God than the primary and indispensable first step before he shows up.

WHEN THE MOLD DOESN'T FIT

Finally, I wondered why I kept running across so many godly people who felt so ungodly.

I now realize it had more to do with our faulty definitions of spirituality than anything else. In most cases, these people felt like spiritual failures not because they were far from God, but because they'd been unable to live up to generally accepted measures of spirituality.

They had stalled out in Leviticus each time they tried to read through the Bible. They were kinetic types who found extended prayer not only unfulfilling, but nearly torturous. Or extroverts who'd bought one of those fancy leather journals, but never got around to putting anything in it.

Mostly, they were regular folks who for whatever reason didn't fit the mold too well. They tried it, but sadly found it didn't work for them.

A CONTRARIAN'S PERSPECTIVE

As we explore what it means to know God and experience God-pleasing spirituality in a way that's accessible for everyone, you'll notice that we take some admittedly contrarian paths. But rest assured, they're not contrarian for contrarian's sake. If that were the case, they would have no value.

Contrarian thinking for the sake of being contrarian is an arrogant waste of time. Claiming that the world is flat just because everyone else says it's round is a fool's playground.

There's nothing wrong with conventional wisdom when it's right. And most of the time it is.

But when it's not, someone has to speak up.

Contrarian thinking at its best simply asks, *Is that really true?* And it speaks up when the politically correct answer or conventional wisdom doesn't match reality—when things don't work the way everyone says they do or thinks they do.

> Contrarian thinking at its best simply asks, Is that really true?

Contrarianism also represents a much-needed form of candor. It dares to speak the unspeakable, to voice what others may have been thinking but for some reason have been afraid to say out loud. Much like a young boy standing by the roadside asking, "Why is the emperor butt naked?"

That's the kind of thinking, candor, and courage I hope you'll find on the pages to follow.

My bet is that you'll find some of it incredibly freeing, some of it annoying, some maddening, and some of it still open to debate.

I also hope you'll find yourself thinking more than a few times, "You know, I always thought the same thing—but I didn't know anybody else did too."

CHAPTER TWO

RELIGION OR RELATIONSHIP?

CHRISTIANS ARE FOND OF CLAIMING that Christianity is not a religion, that it's a *personal relationship* with Jesus.

Sounds great; has a nice ring to it. In fact, it was one of the first "witnessing" sound bites I learned to use when sharing my faith. It was supposed to silence and maybe even convert those who dared to question the uniqueness of Jesus and Christianity.

I spouted the line for years. But in all honesty, I had no idea what it meant. And upon further reflection, I don't think a lot of other Christians do either.

Just look at our models of spiritual formation. Almost all our books, seminars, workshops, and programs are heavily weighted toward religious practice and self-discipline. They show us how to do religion in hopes that it will produce relationship.

RELIGION AND RELATIONSHIP

But religion and relationships have little to nothing in common.

Religion places a major emphasis on rules and rituals that are supposed to either manipulate God or earn his favor. The tell-tale mark of religion is easy to spot. It's a one-size-fits-all approach to spirituality: "Follow our rules, fulfill our rituals, and God (or the gods) will be pleased and placated."

Relationships are completely different. No one-size-fits-all recipe can guarantee a great relationship. Whether we're talking about husband and wife, close friends, co-workers, or parent and child, every relationship is different. No two are ever exactly alike. What builds and sustains one is often of no value in another.

MARRIED TO MATT

After my friend Matt lost his wife, few of us were surprised when he later remarried. He'd had an amazing marriage with his first wife. They were "one" in the truest sense of the word. He loved being married, and the opportunity to be so again was too tempting to pass up.

Sure enough, he struck gold twice. Life with his second wife was every bit as great as life with his first.

But it was different.

Long walks in the park and quiet evenings of reading together were replaced with a more adventuresome lifestyle. While sex started in the kitchen for wife number one, helping to clean up after dinner did nothing for wife number two. But a day of canoeing or riding bikes together…well, you get the picture.

Now, imagine if Matt had insisted on doing marriage with his second wife exactly as with the first—the same communication patterns, the same special moments, the same interpersonal rituals. All of us in his inner circle would have told him he was nuts. Before long, a marriage counselor would have told him the same thing, though a bit more diplomatically.

Obviously Matt is just one person, the same guy in each of his two marriages. But his wives weren't the same. And that's the reason each marriage took on a flavor and style of its own. No two relationships will ever be exactly alike because no two people are exactly alike. Each relationship has its own dance and drama, played out according to the unique strengths, needs, and personalities of the partners..

> Something tells me God doesn't just put up with our differences, he savors them—and adapts to them

It's no different in our relationship with God. Certainly *he's* always the same, but we're sure different. And something tells me God doesn't just put up with our differences, he savors them—and adapts to them. After all, he's the one who created all these unique traits, even those we aren't so fond of in others.

TWO BROTHERS

My brother Bob and I couldn't have been more different. As we were growing up, I'm not sure we understood or appreciated each other all that much.

I was a jock and a wannabe hippie. Bob was musically gifted and a wannabe cop. I still remember the day I came home from basketball practice and found him lying on the bed reading *How to Set Up Police Roadblocks.* He was two years younger, and I was genuinely worried for his future. From my vantage point as a long-hair, cops were hardly in vogue. Our peers called them "pigs."

I wondered if Bob would ever get married, ever have cool friends, ever find a job he could be proud of.

He was concerned about the same things. Only not about himself, but about me.

Bob instinctively knew that the ability to hit an occasional jump shot wouldn't do me much good in the long run. And while my long hair, Levis, and tie-dyed tank tops might have made a strong fashion statement, he knew I'd have to get a job someday—and dress like it.

I'm sure he wondered if I'd ever stay married, ever have friends who were sober, ever find a job I could keep.

Somehow we both made it. Bob has had a long and successful career in police work, rising to the highest ranks of leadership and impacting people for good and for God all along the way. I too found a niche and a place in society that's been far more successful and impactful than he or any of us would have guessed at the time.

ONE DAD

In the middle of all this was my dad. Strangely, he not only loved us both, he liked us just the way we were.

A look back at our relationship with him as an earthly father can reveal some powerful insights into God's relationship with his own spiritual sons and daughters.

Actually, Mom and Dad had three kids. Besides Bob and me, there's a younger sister named Linda who, like many third-borns, gets along with everybody. Though she's a great sister, she kind of messes up the analogy here, so we'll just mostly leave her out for now. (Please don't tell her.)

ONE SET OF HOUSE RULES

Bob and I were so different that as soon as my folks could afford it, they added on an extra bedroom so we wouldn't have to share. I think they feared a homicide under their roof otherwise.

But no matter how different we were as siblings, we shared one thing in common: a set of house rules that Dad laid down for all of us.

The rules were simple and clear. Stay out of trouble. Do your homework—at least most of it. Be home before curfew, go to church, and make sure Mom or Dad knows where you are and who you're with. Obviously, there were a few more rules, but the key point is that when it came to house rules, they were the same for everybody.

And that's just the way it is with our heavenly Father. The house rules are the clear commands of Scripture. It doesn't matter if I'm the forgiving type or not; the house rule is "Forgive." It doesn't matter if everyone else in my industry fudges the truth; honesty is the house rule. And even if my peers think I'm crazy, repressed, or whatever, if I'm not married, sex is not an option. It's a house rule.

> **God's house rules aren't hard to figure out.**

God's house rules aren't hard to figure out. Anyone who reads the Bible, listens to it, or asks someone who knows it to help them out will have no trouble figuring out what the basic house rules are.

That doesn't mean we'll always agree with God's rules. Like kids in an earthly household, we'll sometimes question Dad's wisdom. We'll think his rules are arbitrary, restrictive, or out of touch. But no matter how much we might struggle with any given rule at any given time, we all know what the rules are. They're neither hidden nor hard to decipher.

UNIQUELY DIFFERENT WAYS OF RELATING

Along with the basic house rules for all of us, Dad and Mom also had a flexible set of guidelines and expectations tailored to who we were and how we responded as individuals. A propensity to procrastinate might result in a homework-first, play-later schedule for one of us, while good grades would generate a get-it-done-whenever-you-want freedom for the other.

Along with differing rules based on our unique needs,

responses, and personalities, we also experienced our relationship with Dad in very different ways.

I'm talkative. If I think it, it won't be long before you hear it. This is not a new thing; I'm told I was always that way. Growing up I talked—and talked. And as far as I was concerned, based upon my own experiences with Dad, the key to a great relationship with your father is to talk about stuff, sharing your thoughts about anything from politics to religion to sports—especially USC football.

He was a huge Trojan fan, and so was I. We went to every home game together for years. He seemed to delight in telling me stories about the good old days, the great players and plays. I loved hearing about them and trying to convince him that the players of my youth were better than the players of his youth.

In addition, I played basketball throughout high school. The result was a plethora of shared experiences built around the joys and heartbreaks of each season.

My brother was more reserved. He was far less likely to debate an issue or even discuss it. At that point in time, sports weren't much of an interest either.

But he did have a knack for music and a keen eye for irony. As he grew older he became a great storyteller—really funny. I don't know why, but cops always have great stories. Maybe they run into better material than the rest of us.

Anyway, Bob didn't relate to Dad by reading a book or an article on the USC Trojans and discussing it. He seldom argued politics, and never shared the ups and downs of a championship basketball season.

But he had no problem developing a great relationship with Dad. A shared interest in music and travel, a common eye for the ironic, and Bob's track record of accomplishments in school and his chosen career gave Dad plenty of reasons to be proud of him—

and plenty of ways to connect.

Now, imagine the absurdity of either Bob or me trying to tell the other, "The real secret to a great relationship with Dad is to relate to him exactly the way *I* relate to him." Or worse, "The only way to Dad's heart is *my* way."

The truth is that our dad related to each of us differently. He still does. There may be only one of him, but there are three of us (counting Linda—you know, the left-out sister), and we all connect and stay connected in ways that are as different as our unique personalities, strengths, and needs.

> No two relationships with God will ever be exactly alike.

And that's exactly how it is with our heavenly Father. If we want to know him, really know him, it can only be done through developing a personal relationship. And no two personal relationships will ever be exactly alike.

Our one-size-fits-all discipleship and spirituality recipes have to go. We must recognize them for what they are—mere religion in the guise of relationship.

Family differences—a brief fly-by:

Accept him whose faith is weak, without passing judgment on disputable matters. One man's faith allows him to eat everything, but another man, whose faith is weak, eats only vegetables. The man who eats everything must not look down on him who does not, and the man who does not eat everything must not condemn the man who does, for God has accepted him. Who are you to judge someone else's servant? To his own master he stands or falls. And he will stand, for the Lord is able to make him stand. One man considers one day more sacred than another; another man considers every day alike. Each one should be fully convinced in his own mind. He who regards one day as special, does so to the Lord. He who eats meat, eats to the Lord, for he gives thanks to God; and he who abstains, does so to the Lord and gives thanks to God. (Romans 14:1–6)

Therefore let us stop passing judgment on one another. Instead, make up your mind not to put any stumbling block or obstacle in your brother's way. (Romans 14:13)

For the kingdom of God is not a matter of eating and drinking, but of righteousness, peace and joy in the Holy Spirit, because anyone who serves Christ in this way is pleasing to God and approved by men. (Romans 14:17–18)

So whatever you believe about these things keep between yourself and God. Blessed is the man who does not condemn himself by what he approves. (Romans 14:22)

Accept one another, then, just as Christ accepted you, in order to bring praise to God. (Romans 15:7)

CHAPTER THREE

JESUS OR JOHN?

LET'S ADMIT IT. Most of us think that if other people only knew what we know and experienced what we've experienced, they'd pretty much see life the way we do.

I call it the Blank Slate Theory.

It's based on the assumption that there's only one logical response to any body of information or set of experiences. And of course, *our* response is the logical response.

In a culture that highly values tolerance, few of us want to admit to thinking that way. But it's exactly how most of us think most of the time.

THE THINGS THAT DIVIDE US

Just look at the way we critique and try to change those who see and respond to life in ways radically different from our own. We assail their logic and belittle their experiences, confident that the only explanation for their differences is a lack of exposure to information we possess or experiences we've encountered.

You can see it in families. A dad who loves camping, hunting,

35

and fishing gives the wife and kids fifteen reasons why outdoor living is good for them, plus a story about how much he hated it until he tried it.

They try it.

They still prefer Disneyland.

You can see it in our political dialogues. We throw data at each other, convinced that once the other side stops and listens, they'll get it. Neither side seems to accept the possibility that given the exact same info and experiences, they still might disagree.

When it comes to spirituality, we do the same thing. We have a hard time accepting the validity of expressions of the Christian faith that are radically different than our own.

Depending on where we are on the theological and personality spectrum, the other guys are too sheltered or too worldly, too materialistic or too idealistic, sold out or compromised, zealous or crazy.

But the truth is, we aren't born as a blank slate. We're all radically different from birth. The same information and experiences that shaped us into who we are can produce a very different worldview, theological perspective, and pattern of spirituality when seen through the lens of another.

That's not to say there's no such thing as absolute spiritual truth—or that it resides only in the eyes of the beholder. The Bible spells out plenty of things in black and white—certainly all the important stuff.

But that's not what usually divides us. Mostly it's the things the Bible *doesn't* nail down that we fight over. It's the practical outworking of biblical implications and principles that sends us down drastically different paths.

Let's be real. We may know in our head that each Christian has a unique assignment from God. But when the assignments produce radically different lifestyles and approaches to spirituality, we have a difficult time validating both.

This is nothing new. It's always been that way. Even the followers of Jesus and John the Baptist had to work their way through it.

WHO ARE YOU?

John the Baptist was a weird bird. At least, most of us would think so if we were to run into him in real life instead of the safety of a Bible lesson.

The cousin of Jesus, he was a wilderness-dwelling ascetic who dressed in itchy camel's hair, ate a strange diet of locusts and wild honey, and greeted the large crowds who flocked to hear him with a harsh message of repentance and a call to be baptized.

When the theologians and religious leaders came to check him out, he ticked them off by calling them names and insisting that they, too, needed to get right with God or face judgment.

His core message was that both the kingdom of God and the Messiah were coming soon. So when Jesus finally showed up, John baptized him and publicly proclaimed him to be the One. After that, Jesus went off to begin his public ministry.

But later, when stories of Jesus' exploits and teaching made their way back to John, he responded in a strange way. He dispatched two of his personal aides to ask Jesus if he was indeed the Messiah, or if they should wait for someone else.

Now remember, this was the same man who had earlier baptized Jesus and personally heard God the Father announce, "This is my Son in whom I am well pleased!"[1] So why in the world would John send two of his followers to ask Jesus whether he was the Messiah?

I have a hard time imagining that it was because of the stories of Jesus' great power and miracles. Those stories fit nicely with everyone's expectations of a messiah.

My guess is that it had more to do with the *way* Jesus did his ministry. John had heard the rumors of amazing power, but he was also sure to have heard stories of Jesus hanging out with sinners, turning water into wine, and generally rejecting the lifestyle commonly expected of a prophet and holy man.

John was left to wonder: Is this man who we thought he was? And if so, why is he acting this way?

SHOW HIM THE FRUIT

It's interesting to me that Jesus didn't answer John's emissaries with a discourse on how he fulfilled messianic prophecies or a defense of his actions and ministry style.

Instead, he simply continued doing what he'd been doing all along—healing the sick, casting out evil spirits, and turning hearts back to God. Then he told John's two friends to go back and tell John exactly what they'd seen.

Jesus was sending a clear message. They'd been looking at the wrong things. The proof of his messiahship was not to be found in the style and format of his ministry; it was to be found in the fruit of his ministry—God's power working mightily in the lives of many.

JOHN'S LEGACY

As John's two messengers left, the crowd must have been wondering what Jesus thought of John, especially in light of his audacity in sending these two followers to publicly question his credentials.

Jesus responded with glowing praise. John the Baptist, he said, was a great man and a prophet.

Most of the crowd probably agreed. They had flocked to John and now were flocking to Jesus. But this answer didn't sit too well with the theologians and trained religious leaders.

John or Jesus?

[John the Ascetic]—In those days John the Baptist came, preaching in the Desert of Judea and saying, "Repent, for the kingdom of heaven is near." ...John's clothes were made of camel's hair, and he had a leather belt around his waist. His food was locusts and wild honey. People went out to him from Jerusalem and all Judea and the whole region of the Jordan. Confessing their sins, they were baptized by him in the Jordan River. (Matthew 3:1–6)

[Jesus the Party Animal]—While Jesus was having dinner at Matthew's house, many tax collectors and "sinners" came and ate with him and his disciples. When the Pharisees saw this, they asked his disciples, "Why does your teacher eat with tax collectors and 'sinners'?" On hearing this, Jesus said, "It is not the healthy who need a doctor, but the sick. But go and learn what this means: 'I desire mercy, not sacrifice.' For I have not come to call the righteous, but sinners." Then John's disciples came and asked him, "How is it that we and the Pharisees fast, but your disciples do not fast?" (Matthew 9:10–14)

[The Both/And of God's Kingdom, in Jesus' Words]— To what, then, can I compare the people of this generation? What are they like? They are like children sitting in the marketplace and calling out to each other: "We played the flute for you, and you did not dance; we sang a dirge, and you did not cry." For John the Baptist came neither eating bread nor drinking wine, and you say, "He has a demon." The Son of Man came eating and drinking, and you say, "Here is a glutton and a drunkard, a friend of tax collectors and 'sinners.'" But wisdom is proved right by all her children. (Luke 7:31–35)

They'd rejected John as a kook, a crazy man who didn't understand their spiritually privileged position as descendants of Abraham, a heretic who wanted Jews to be baptized like common Gentiles.

To make matters worse, when they'd gone out to the wilderness to investigate first-hand the phenomena of his large crowds and teaching, he greeted them less than warmly: "You brood of vipers! Who warned you to flee from the coming wrath?"[2] Hardly the friendly greeting you'd expect at the ministry information booth.

IMPOSSIBLE TO PLEASE

These same religious leaders also blew off Jesus as a rogue rabbi, albeit one with unusual spiritual powers—powers which some of them dismissed as coming from Satan himself.

Finally, Jesus had had enough. He turned to the Pharisees and teachers of the law and nailed them with a pointed analogy. As we read the Bible's account of it,[3] we can almost feel his frustration at their arrogance and cocksure definitions of what God-pleasing spirituality should look like.

Jesus compared his and John's detractors to spoiled children calling out to one another in the marketplace, never satisfied with anything or anyone. When someone played the flute, the instrument of celebration and rejoicing, they wouldn't dance. When someone sang a funeral dirge, they wouldn't cry. No matter what, they couldn't be pleased.

They had responded to John's ascetic ministry of self-denial and isolation by claiming he had a demon.

And they responded to Jesus' accessibility and openness by branding him as a party animal—a glutton, a drunkard, and too close a friend of sinners.

Jesus told them they had it all wrong. He and John the Baptist were both pleasing to the Father, despite the radical differences in their approach to ministry and lifestyle. And the wisdom of each of their paths was proved right by the children or fruit of their ministry.

Jesus was making it clear that the most important thing in pleasing God is not a particular approach to spirituality or style of ministry; it's the fruit that matters, the end results produced by our life and ministry.

And on that account, both Jesus and John passed with flying colors.

> The most important thing in pleasing God is not a particular approach to spirituality or style of ministry; what matters is the fruit

LESSONS FOR TODAY

Frankly, it's hard to imagine any two people or ministries more polar opposites than Jesus and John.

One lived in isolation waiting for people to come to him; the other traveled from town to town seeking out sinners. One followed a strict religious diet and fulfilled the rigors of a Nazarite vow; the other attended parties, lots of parties, and was known for turning water into fine wine.

Their differences were so great that even their followers were confused. John's guys wondered how Jesus could possibly be the Messiah if he followed a path so different from the path they walked. And Jesus' disciples were equally confused about John. How could one so unlike their master possibly be pleasing to the heavenly Father?

Yet Jesus made it clear: The Father was greatly pleased with both.

COULD THE SAME THING be happening today?

Could God be pleased with those whose walk with him is as different from ours as John's was from that of Jesus?

Could the patterns, disciplines, and paths of spirituality we hold so dear be far less important than the fruit they produce?

Is it possible that someone whose journey includes choices, practices, and a lifestyle far different from our own actually knows God as well as or better than we do?

If the words of Jesus mean anything, the answer is a resounding *yes*.

In his critique of John, the Pharisees, and his own ministry, Jesus was saying something most Christian leaders seem to miss: It's the *fruit* that matters.

That should forever put to bed our attempts to create a one-size-fits-all spirituality. It should silence much of our criticisms of one another. And if properly understood, it should lead to a genuine celebration of our diversity in calling and in our expressions of faith.

John or Jesus?

The answer is *both*.

CHAPTER FOUR

IS IT A SIN TO BE AVERAGE?

Is GOD-PLEASING SPIRITUALITY supposed to morph us into some sort of super saint?

As a new Christian I would have answered, "Of course."

All my faith heroes were mountain-moving, charge-the-hill warriors for God. There was no mistaking the underlying message: If God ever got hold of all of me, or of anyone else for that matter…then watch out, world!

Somehow, somewhere, I picked up the idea that we're all called to do great things for God; that the godlier we become, the more we'll be transformed into spiritual Bravehearts, serving God and marshalling others to do the same.

It sounds good. It's motivational, as long as you're the kind of person who dreams big dreams.

But what if you're more the retiring type? What if you've never dreamed of turning your world upside down for God—or your neighborhood for that matter?

What if your idea of a great life is a quiet life?

Does that mean something is seriously wrong with your

spirituality? Or could it be that's how God made you, and the rest of us will just have to learn to deal with it?

IS BEING AVERAGE A SIN?

I would say that many (if not most) Christian leaders, whether they ever say it aloud or not, think something is spiritually wrong with a low-drive Christian.

That's because leaders tend to project their passion for advancing the causes of the kingdom onto everyone else. Since they've heard their own call so clearly, they assume anyone who doesn't share the same passions and vision must not know God very well—or at least, must not be listening to what God has to say.

That's exactly how I felt until God brought two remarkable people into my life. They weren't remarkable for what they accomplished; they were remarkable for who they were. Both were as godly in character as anyone I've ever met, and neither had a leadership bone in them.

What's more, when it came time to charge the hill, they opted to serve in the supply line. When challenged to sign up for our programs, work their way up the system, or join us in what we saw as bold steps of faith, they smiled and politely demurred.

On one hand, they failed to match up to my image of what a sold-out, on-fire Christian should look like. To most people, they appeared to be pretty average folks. Not a lot of drive, not a lot of accomplishments.

On the other hand, when it came to their character, relationships, and integrity, they were two of the most Christlike people I'd ever met.

And that caused me to start wondering if perhaps my definition of sold-out Christianity was seriously flawed. To put it more bluntly, I began to wonder if there was room in the kingdom for mediocrity. Could someone be average and still please God?

What if God didn't want everyone to be turned into a leader and a hill-charging spiritual warrior? Could he possibly be pleased with simple folks who loved God, loved their family and friends, then died without ever doing (or wanting to do) anything outstandingly significant?

The more I mulled this over, and the more closely I examined the Bible, the more convinced I became that the answer was yes. Mediocrity was actually an option—and for some, a God-pleasing option.

It had to be. Because if it's impossible to be below average and please God, we have a BIG problem on our hands. Whatever we're measuring, and by whatever measure we use, half of us will always be on the wrong side of the average line, by the very definition of it.

Now, I know that's grating for some. It smacks of devaluing the power of God, ignoring the great needs in our world, and neglecting the unction of the Holy Spirit. How can a God-filled and God-led person remain average—or worse, below average? Why would anyone want to settle for anything less than high-impact significance?

But the fact is, our aversion to mediocrity comes more out of our cultural values than out of the Bible.

God-pleasing spirituality may or may not go hand in hand with spiritual leadership. If you don't believe me, check out the stories of King Saul and Samson. Both were powerful leaders in God's kingdom, but neither seemed to know him all that well.

YES YOU CAN!

We live in a culture of perceived opportunity. The American ethos in particular fosters the idea that we can do anything or be anything we set our minds to, if we want it badly enough and are willing to pay the price. Christians add in the faith factor, and suddenly we assume nothing is impossible.

We love rags-to-riches stories and always believe a pauper can become a king. No one wants to kill a dream—to tell someone, "No, you can't." So we don't.

But the truth is, some things *can't* be done, and some people are destined to be below average on the spiritual leadership and impact scale. That doesn't mean something's wrong. It just means they weren't called to be high-impact leaders.

The result of the you-can-do-anything-with-God myth is that those who score way above average on the giftedness, intensity, or influence meter often become puffed up with pride. While they may mouth politically correct words about giving God all the credit, most don't really believe it. They think they had a great deal to do with it.

And can you blame them? In a system where significant spiritual impact is available to anyone willing to pay the price, those who have it must be more committed than those who don't.

On the other side are lots of good and godly folks left to lick the wounds of countless well-intentioned but spiritually hurtful sermons, books, and seminars calling them to be something they know in their heart of hearts they can never be—and have no desire to be, if truth be known.

I'm not talking about cold and lukewarm Christians who practice casual spirituality and open-handed disobedience. I'm talking about wonderful people of integrity and obedience to God's word who simply don't register much on the intensity or impact meter—and never will.

THE COBBLER'S JOURNEY

These people are what I call "cobblers in Corinth."

It's a phrase I coined years ago while reading through the New Testament in search of all I could learn about the ministry of the early church and the church-planting efforts of the apostle Paul.

The more I read, the more I was struck by how much my leadership bias had blinded me to the reality of life as a first-century Christian.

I'd always assumed that Timothy, Titus, Silas, and the rest of Paul's missionary partners represented the standard fruit of his ministry. I paid close attention to everything they did and every bit of instruction and advice Paul gave them. To my thinking, this represented what every Christian under my leadership needed to know and what they all, ideally, would become.

> Guys like Timothy and Titus were not the standard fruit of Paul's ministry.

But I was missing the blindingly obvious. Timothy and Titus were not the standard fruit of Paul's ministry. They were the rare and unusual; they were the next generation of leaders.

The vast majority of the people Paul led to Christ, and the vast majority of people in the churches he planted, never became leaders or joined Paul on one of his missionary journeys. They were farmers and merchants, mothers and fathers, sons and daughters who quietly lived out changed lives through Christ.

They included my "cobbler in Corinth," the shoemaker who stopped visiting the temple prostitutes, became scrupulously honest in his business dealings, and treated his wife and children with a love and respect unknown in the pagan and Roman world.

And though he may have never planted a church, spent hours in study or solitude, or courageously preached on a street corner, he did cross the finish line still loving and following

Jesus. And in God's eyes, I have to believe, his life was a win—a big win.

In fact, over time, it was the "cobblers" left behind in Corinth who turned the ancient world upside down, just as much as the missionaries bouncing from town to town. Both were needed. Someone had to spread the word; someone had to stay behind and live it out.

As the majesty of these "cobblers in Corinth" became more evident to me, it radically altered my approach to ministry. It's not that I stopped focusing on leaders and leadership development. That's too important to ignore. But I stopped trying to make *everyone* into a leader.

DRIVE-BY GUILTINGS

Let's be honest. In many of our churches, modern-day cobblers are ignored or, even worse, assailed as unproductive drains on the kingdom.

If you're a cobbler-type Christian, you know what I mean. You've been hammered with countless sermons on the Parable of the Talents, usually interpreted to mean you're not doing enough. You've been exhorted to aggressively preach the gospel. You've been force-fed a diet of spiritual disciplines, skills, and biblical knowledge all designed to make you into the one thing you've never wanted to be: a leader.

You've probably also been bombarded with drive-by guiltings—not for your failure to obey Christ's commands or be changed by the Holy Spirit, but simply for failing to match up to the conventional hard-charging, highly disciplined, and deeply introspective definitions of spirituality.

No wonder so many of us simply give up. We've never seen a model of spirituality that actually works for us.

——

I WISH I'D SEEN this earlier in my ministry. I certainly should have. My parents were the quintessential cobblers in Corinth. They didn't teach lots of Bible studies, talk to total strangers about Christ, lead mission trips, house the homeless, or do anything all that spectacular for God.

They went to church, hosted an occasional Bible study, and served on a few committees and even an elder board or two. But when it came to stretching themselves beyond their comfort zone or jumping through all the hoops a committed Christian was supposed to jump through, they were more likely to opt out than in.

My mom must have started reading through the New Testament thirty times—usually stalling out somewhere toward the end of Matthew or the beginning of Mark. Dad was a more disciplined reader, but as for all the other standard spiritual disciplines, he and mom would start and stop like a fat man on a diet.

All they did was live a life of obedience with grace and dignity. All they accomplished was raising three children who would walk with Jesus as adults—and who, strangely, would all have gifts of teaching and leadership.

All they did was love and know God…model a quiet life without hypocrisy…and bear the fruit to prove it.

In my mind, they were not only spiritual, they were spiritual giants.

> Make it your ambition to lead a quiet life, to mind your own business and to work with your hands, just as we told you, so that your daily life may win the respect of outsiders and so that you will not be dependent on anybody. *(1 Thessalonians 4:11–12)*

A FINAL THOUGHT

For those of us who are cobbler-in-Corinth Christians, the key to knowing God on a truly personal level and experiencing a genuine God-pleasing spirituality may well begin with the vanquishing of all the old tapes and voices calling us to be something we're not.

Instead, we must learn to listen to the still small voice of the Spirit as he calls and equips us to be a better us, rather than a poor imitation of someone else.

For those of us who are leader types, we can expect to find plenty of help for our spiritual journey. We're the prized prospect, the kind of Christian most churches and ministry organizations encourage and motivate best.

We need to keep at it; we're vital to the future of the church and God's kingdom. But we also need to work hard not to project our personality and calling on everyone else.

The goal of spirituality is not to lead—it's to know and please God.

2

HOW DOES SPIRITUAL GROWTH HAPPEN?

CHAPTER FIVE

THE CASE FOR MEANDERING

HAVE YOU NOTICED that most of our programs and models for spiritual development follow a strict linear pattern? Step one, followed by step two, and so on.

Yet, if we stop and look back at our own spiritual journey, few of us will find anything close to a neatly laid out linear path. For most of us, the road to spiritual growth and maturity is more like a meandering path punctuated by occasional stretches of unexpected twists and turns.

So why do we place such a great emphasis on sequential steps and an orderly progression in our discipleship programs and models? I believe it's primarily because linear models and programs are much easier to design and administrate.

In reality, most spiritual growth happens on a haphazard need-to-grow or need-to-know basis. As life happens, we're suddenly confronted by the need for personal growth or more biblical information in an area of life that up to now hasn't seemed all that important.

THE NEED TO GROW

A number of years ago, my wife was diagnosed with breast cancer. It was invasive, fast-growing, and falsely diagnosed at first. By the time we realized what we were dealing with, and had scheduled and completed the surgery, all signs pointed toward stage-four cancer.

In the darkest days, when it looked like she might not make it, we both experienced a new sense of urgency to fully understand and live out the implications of God's sovereignty. It was a classic need-to-grow moment.

Prior to that, the sovereignty of God was a topic to preach or a doctrine to debate—but hardly one we desperately needed to grab hold of and put to work in our lives.

Though this was a course neither of us wanted to take, we tackled it with gusto. Deep discussion about life and death, our future dreams, and a crisis completely out of our control became normal fare. Our prayer life ratcheted up a notch or two. I found myself journaling and reexamining key Scriptures.

The end result was that a once dry, overly academic subject took on new life, eventually becoming a rock we could both stand on.

> Life happens, growth kicks in...but the curriculum order is seldom the same for any two people.

It's a pattern I've since seen over and over. Life happens, and growth kicks in. But the order of the curriculum is seldom the same for any two people.

I wish I could foresee the future and prepare for what's coming next. But I can't. Only God knows, and he's not in the habit of emailing me the upcoming schedule for review—most likely because if he did, I'd too often decide to skip the course.

THE NEED TO KNOW

Sometimes life presents a situation where our primary need is simply for more information. We might need to know what the Bible says to do in a specific case. We might need a godly or eternal perspective. We might need a better understanding of a biblical doctrine in order to correctly discern between competing claims of truth and error.

As a new Christian I found myself in a work situation where I was asked to lie. It was a job that paid by the hour but demanded a set amount of work within the allotted time frame.

This meant everyone was expected to work "off the clock." It was explained to me that we were being paid by the task no matter how short or long it took. If we finished early we could go home and have someone else clock out for us. If we didn't get done in time, we punched out, then finished the job.

After I'd worked there about a year, an investigator from corporate headquarters came for a visit. He was going around asking each of us if we'd ever worked off the clock.

I didn't know how I should respond. Fifty others had already answered no. If I told the truth, I would get all of them in trouble, possibly lose my job, and hurt our store. Though I considered honesty the best policy, I wasn't so sure it applied to a complex situation like this.

Since I was the last person to be interviewed, I had time to ask my Bible study group what to do.

They showed me verse after verse that called for honesty no matter what. Enough that all my "Yeah, buts…" lost their sway.

It was a classic need-to-know situation. Once my friends showed me the Scriptures, I knew what to do. I did the right thing. And from then on, I carried with me a knowledge base to guide me through any and all similar situations.

HOW WE LEARN—WHAT WE REMEMBER

If passing along information is an important part of spiritual growth (and I believe it is), we might want to take into consideration what makes some of it so sticky—and what makes other things slippery and hard to recall.

Our church offers a class for new Christians called Christianity 101. It's designed to cover the basics for those who've recently stepped over the line to follow Jesus. In it, we teach the standard curriculum: The deity of Christ, what it means to be a Christian, introduction to the Bible, the Holy Spirit, the Trinity, and so on.

But let's be honest. Though the outline of topics might look great in a proposal to a Christian education committee, in the mind of a typical new Christian, some of those obligatory topics are baffling.

For instance, in every 101-type curriculum I've seen, there's a section devoted to the deity of Christ and the Trinity. Ours is no different.

But from the perspective of a new Christian, a discourse on the Trinity isn't enlightening; it's bewildering—often leaving the new believer more confused at the end of the class than he was at the beginning.

Not that the Trinity is unimportant. It's very important. But it's also a subject that even trained theologians have long struggled to comprehend. What chance does someone new to the Bible have to grasp it—especially in their first days of acquaintance with Jesus and the Scriptures?

But we still teach it anyway. Why? Because it's a foundational truth, and in a linear approach to discipleship we assume that whatever is foundational must be taught first. Even if those we teach it to have no idea what it means or why it's important.

Yet for most of us, there does come a time when what the Bible has to say about the Trinity and the relationship of the Father, Son, and Holy Spirit becomes suddenly important. It's when a Jehovah's Witness stands on the porch or takes up residence in the cubicle next door. It's when someone tries to tell us Jesus never claimed to be God and shouldn't be worshiped as God.

Now, if our linear approaches to discipleship really worked, we'd all pull our Christianity 101 notebook off the shelf, review what we've been taught, and be ready to answer and defend the truth.

But our typical response is telling. No matter how many detailed notes on the subject we've stuffed into our Christianity 101 notebook, the first time we're confronted by a cultist, most of us (whether a new or long-time Christian) end up turning to someone else for help. We call on a perceived expert within our realm of contacts and ask for assistance in understanding and responding to the cultist's accusations.

The reason is simple. The information we received in the classroom didn't stick. It might have been clearly spelled out in the pages of a syllabus; we might even find it and review what we wrote down. But in most cases the words are without meaning—mere scribbles with little chance of standing up to the well-trained apologists on the front porch.

> Even incredibly vital information doesn't stick unless we're convinced that it's important to know.

Information, even incredibly vital information, doesn't stick unless we're convinced at the time it's delivered that it's *important* to know—or at least will be someday.

That's why so many of our information-based Bible studies and linear discipleship programs look a lot better on paper than they do in real life. In theory, they're profoundly life-changing. In reality, their impact is often minimal—and whatever changes they produce quickly fade.

AM I DONE YET?

Our overemphasis on linear models of spiritual growth also tends to produce another unintended consequence. Once we've finished a course or program, we think we're done.

It's rather like finishing a class in college. We think, *I've got it mastered and I have the transcript to prove it.* At least until our kids start asking for help with their homework. That's when we realize that what we thought was mastery was only familiarity—a familiarity with little or no stickiness.

In the same way, many of us feel like we've mastered a biblical topic or spiritual discipline when we've taken a course on it, heard a sermon, or attended a seminar. But in reality we don't *know* it; we're just familiar with it.

On top of that, spirituality is not something we master anyway. It's a lifelong quest of getting closer—not getting "there." Perfect mastery is no more attainable in spirituality than it is in marriage, parenting, friendship, or any other relationship. They're all like peeling an onion; there's always another layer to deal with.

Isn't that what the apostle Paul implies when he looks at his own spiritual journey and says that he hasn't already arrived, that

Not that I have already obtained all this, or have already been made perfect, but I press on to take hold of that for which Christ Jesus took hold of me. Brothers, I do not consider myself yet to have taken hold of it.... All of us who are mature should take such a view of things. And if on some point you think differently, that too God will make clear to you. Only let us live up to what we have already attained. (Philippians 3:12–16) he continues to press on and strain for a goal that's still out of reach?[4] Here was a guy writing the Bible! You'd think if anyone could lay claim to having mastered spirituality, it would be him. But Paul knew better. And it indicates to me that you and I probably won't reach the point any time soon of having spiritually arrived.

PROCESS OR CURRICULUM?

This is not to say everything linear is bad or ineffective. I'm simply suggesting that the linear approach is way overrated and overused.

If you're one of the rare straight-line kind of Christians whose primary means of growth has been line-by line, and if you benefit from linear models—by all means keep at it. It's the path that works best for you.

But if you're not so straight-line, don't worry about your meandering or where you should go next. You'll get where you need to be as long as you stay on the path and look first to God and Scripture when a need-to-grow or need-to-know crisis pops up.

> Don't worry about your meandering or where you should go next. You'll get where you need to be.

In the meantime, don't fret if you go through a dry spell, or if the standard linear programs fail to produce much fruit.

The simple process of meandering through various discipleship options—even in a laissez-faire or stop-and-go fashion—will keep you closely connected and ready to receive the help and information you'll need when a need-to-grow or need-to-know moment hits.

AND FINALLY, for those of us who are spiritual leaders producing or using straight-line linear models of discipleship, we need to ask ourselves a question: Is it because that's how *we've* grown spiritually, or is it simply because they're so much easier to design and administrate?

If it's because they actually worked for us—we need to remember that they won't work for everybody.

If it's only because they're easier to create or administrate, or because everyone else does it that way, then maybe it's time to come clean—to acknowledge that this is not necessarily how most people grow, and that the meandering path is not only the most common path…it's a legitimate path.

CHAPTER SIX

VELCROED FOR GROWTH

LIFE'S MAJOR TRIALS seldom send a memo telling us they're on the way. Instead, like an uninvited guest, they just show up, leaving us no choice but to let them in.

Having watched thousands of people face difficult or confusing circumstances over the years, I've noticed a clear pattern in how things work out.

Those who tend to isolate find it hard to get the help or support they need in a timely manner. Often it's because no one knows. But even when they do, unless it's a heart-wrenching scenario, no one seems to care all that much. Help and support tends to be too little, too late, or perfunctory in nature.

But those who have close and transparent relationships experience a completely different reality. When a crisis hits, they usually find people quick, even eager, to help.

PREPARED FOR CRISIS

Developing close and transparent relationships is an important part of preparing for life's inevitable calamities. It can happen in lots of ways. Going to church helps. Hanging out with other Christians helps. But for most of us, the best tool will be a small cluster of friends who covenant together to meet regularly and share the spiritual journey.

In New Testament days, this kind of small group was called a church. Early Christians had no large buildings to meet in. Most worshiped in what we'd call a "house church." Everyone knew everyone. It was a tough place in which to hide.

Today, with larger churches and the explosive growth of super-sized churches, the closest parallel to the experience of the early church would be a small group or home Bible study where the consistent attendance and smaller size makes it once again possible for everyone to know everyone.

NOW, IT'S HARDLY CONTRARIAN to trumpet small groups as a powerful tool for spiritual growth, and it's hardly contrarian to call for close and transparent relationships.

But it *is* contrarian to actually be in a small group. And you're definitely in the minority if you intentionally maintain close and transparent relationships with more than one or two others.

Just look around. Few churches have anything close to even twenty-five percent of their attenders who consistently meet in

And let us consider how we may spur one another on toward love and good deeds. Let us not give up meeting together, as some are in the habit of doing, but let us encourage one another—and all the more as you see the Day approaching. (Hebrews 10:24–25)

small groups. Surveys show that most people, Christians included (especially men), have only one or two close and transparent relationships. For many, only their spouse has such a relationship with them.

Why then do so many people vouch for the value of a small group while so few actually participate in one?

Besides the standard excuses of time and schedule, there's often another unspoken but equally powerful reason. They've tried it and found it wanting.

The problem is that small groups are usually pushed, sold, and advertised as providing a list of benefits that, frankly, they don't always provide. We sign up, expecting them to do things they don't necessarily do all that well.

As we'll see later, they aren't too effective at preventing sin. They're usually not the greatest vehicle for deep and meaningful Bible study. Nor are they always the source of the great friendships we'd hope for.

While these things may occur, they often don't.

But that shouldn't matter, because the greatest value of being in a small group—or any other form of ongoing, close, and transparent relationships—is found elsewhere. It's found in their ability to provide us with three important accelerators of spiritual growth that are awfully hard to find anywhere else. Yet, ironically, few people even consider these when deciding whether a small group works for them.

THE VELCROING POWER OF
A SMALL GROUP

The primary reason to be in a small group setting is not to learn more biblical information. It's not to develop great friends. It's not even accountability.

It's connectedness. Belonging to a small group, small church, or any other form of close and transparent relationships velcroes me to the people and information I'll need when a need-to-grow or need-to-know crisis shows up.

For instance, when it comes to spiritual growth, the Bible obviously plays a major role. According to the apostle Peter, it contains *everything* we need for life and godliness.[5]

But the problem is that the Bible is a big book. Few of us know all the answers or life principles it contains. If you're like me, you've probably turned to it for help more than once only to be frustrated by the I-know-it's-in-there-somewhere-but-I-can't-find-it syndrome.

That's where those of us who choose to treat Christianity as a team sport have a special advantage. Even when we don't have a clue what, if anything, the Bible says about a particular situation, we invariably know someone who does—or someone who at least knows someone who does.

But those who choose isolation and lone-ranger spirituality have no such luck. The only quick Bible answers they'll ever find are the ones they already know.

Just as important are those times when we need a bear hug to help us hang in there, or a swift kick in the butt to move forward. When we're in a place where relationships are genuine and transparent, there'll always be someone ready to give us what we need.

Not so for those of us who choose to pursue our spirituality primarily in the anonymity of large-group settings or lone-ranger isolation. After all, it's extremely difficult to self-administer a bear hug or a butt-kick.

The unconnected Christian has no one to turn to when he or she needs a shoulder to cry on, or a push in the right direction, or wise advice. And such a person almost certainly has no one to step forward and deliver truth that's hard to hear.

Ultimately, one of the most valuable aspects of a small group is exactly the same as found in a small church: It's a hard place to hide. And that means when life hits, and a need-to-grow or need-to-know situation arises, we're already positioned to get the help we need when we need it.

THE UPSIDE OF PEER PRESSURE

Close and transparent relationships also allow peer pressure to do its good work.

Yes, I said "good work."

Peer pressure gets lots of bad press in the Christian community. That's unfortunate, because peer pressure is neither good nor bad—it just is. It's a potent force that can make us better or worse—or in some cases, cause us to do things that make us look goofy.

> Peer pressure is neither good nor bad—it just is.

Look back at any old yearbook. The pictures don't lie. It's easy to see how we're all greatly impacted by those around us. Like you, I shake my head at what I once thought was cool. With 20/20 hindsight, I realize I was enamored not so much by the style as by who else was wearing it.

We all seem to have a built-in urge to conform. It pulls us toward alignment with what others think, do, and say. Even those who most cherish their nonconformity usually walk in lock-step with other nonconformists.

From beatniks to hippies, Seattle grunge to goth, none of us are as iconoclastic as we'd like to believe.

The biblical warnings about avoiding the wrong crowd are well known. They get lots of attention. So much so that many have taken this avoidance to a ridiculous extreme, producing an unfortunate brand of Christian isolationism that undercuts our ability to impact a world we no longer have any contact with.

Unfortunately, all the bad press has blinded many of us to the positive side of peer pressure. In fact, the negative connotations are so great we often assume that anything done primarily because of outward influence is somehow less praiseworthy or authentic than something done from a purely internal motivation.

Not so.

Here's one Scripture passage where we're pointed to the positive side of peer pressure:

> And let us consider how we may spur one another on toward love and good deeds. Let us not give up meeting together, as some are in the habit of doing, but let us encourage one another—and all the more as you see the Day approaching.[6]

This passage is not just saying we should look for ways to spur one another on to love and good deeds. It's also showing us that one of the most powerful ways to do this is simply to continue meeting together.

Sadly, when I first heard these verses as a young boy, they were used to impress upon me the need to show up and sit in a pew every Sunday. It was as if I'd receive some invisible spiritual value, a sort of mystical spiritual osmosis, just by being present in the crowd.

His divine power has given us everything we need for life and godliness through our knowledge of him who called us by his own glory and goodness. (2 Peter 1:3)

But that's not what these verses are about. They aren't about church attendance; they're about putting the positive power of peer pressure to work. They're about staying connected.

Now, sermons and large gatherings have their place. They can be a powerful catalyst for spiritual insight and growth. If I didn't think so, I wouldn't waste my time preparing and presenting sermons to large gatherings on a weekly basis. But I'm kidding myself if I think they alone can produce long-term, life-changing spirituality. They can't.

The best way to produce that kind of spirituality is to hang around those who are already experiencing it. It's a law of human nature. Over time, we start to think, act, and live like those we spend significant time with.

Those who understand this principle and put it to work find that spiritual growth is just plain easier to come by. It really does "rub off."

THE HONESTY FACTOR

Honesty is another benefit that comes with being closely connected to a small group of Christian friends who share my faith journey.

If I want to grow spiritually, I must be honest enough to let people in on the issues I'm facing and the reality behind the image I portray. I also need friends who are honest enough to tell me the truth—even when I don't want to know it, or it hurts to hear. But that breadth of honesty is hard to come by.

A large church, a mid-sized church, or even a Sunday school class seldom fosters it. As much as we might desire to be real, it's hard to do when strangers are in the room, or people we don't know well enough to be sure they can be trusted with the truth about us.

That's why the conversations in our church parking lots, foyers, and classrooms sound a lot like this:

"How ya doing?"

"Fine. How about you?"

"Fine."

I call it the Church Answer. It's what you'll hear in any hallway in any church on any given Sunday. It doesn't matter how bad things are at work or at home, or how panicked we may be about our future. The answer is always the same: "Fine."

In some ways, that's not all bad. Most folks who ask me how I'm doing don't really want to know. If I actually stopped to tell them, they'd be aghast. All they're really doing is acknowledging my presence. "How ya doing" has become a colloquial phrase meaning, "I see you."

But just the same, we all need some people around us who really want to know how we are—and who we can trust with the truth. People who know us well enough that when they speak into our life, it fits our reality, not our image.

For most of us, this will never be found in a church service or Sunday school class. Why? Because they aren't set up to foster honesty and transparency; they're set up to motivate and pass along information.

Just compare the standard church environment with the characteristics found in a typical small group setting. In which would you be most likely to be open and honest:

In a classroom or a living room?

With twelve people or fifty?

In a group where there's always a new face or one where you know everyone?

That's why small groups foster honesty almost automatically. Their environment practically cries out for it, whereas the ambiance in a typical church setting suppresses transparency in favor of either anonymity or posturing.

NOW, I'M NOT SAYING our large church services have to go. They can serve an incredibly important purpose in transferring information and motivating us to action.

But for genuine and lasting spiritual growth, most of us will have to find a way to move beyond the casual and cautious relationships we so easily settle for.

In this age of worship services too large for us to know the names, much less the lives, of the people we worship with, it's imperative that we somehow find a place where our reality speaks louder than our image, where the upside of positive peer pressure spurs us on to greater heights, and where we're positioned to receive the help we need the moment we need it.

Without that discovery, growth and God-pleasing spirituality will be hard to come by.

All Scripture is God-breathed and is useful for teaching, rebuking, correcting and training in righteousness, so that the man of God may be thoroughly equipped for every good work. (2 Timothy 3:16–17)

CHAPTER SEVEN

THE DIMMER SWITCH
PRINCIPLE

LIKE MOST PASTORS, I have lots of people coming to me for advice.

Church members usually want help with a personal issue—how to deal with a troubled marriage, a wayward child, a financial mess, or a workplace crisis. Because I do a significant amount of speaking and writing on leadership, fellow pastors and business leaders often come with organizational concerns—how to deal with a feisty board, overcome resistance to change, or simply navigate the tricky waters of expansion.

Whatever the problem, my response is always the same. I listen, try to discern the unique aspects of their situation, then apply my best wisdom to whatever it is they're going through.

But some cases are so convoluted there's no easy answer—sometimes no answer at all. When that happens, I'm usually quick to admit I have nothing to offer but a listening ear. There's no need to fake it or pretend I know more than I know.

Other situations are so obvious I know exactly how to solve

them. In those cases, I'm not shy about pointing out to others a prescribed course of action. There's no need to hold back or talk around the issue until they think it's their idea. They've got a sticky problem with an obvious solution, so let's fix it.

THE REALLY TOUGH CASES

Then there's the really tough ones. The cases where people come asking for advice but don't really want it. Unfortunately, it's a lot more common than you might think. Lots of people who ask for advice really want confirmation. They're already convinced they know best.

When these folks ask for advice, it's not so much a genuine search for wisdom as a ritual designed to prove to themselves and others that they've sought outside guidance before going ahead and doing exactly as they please.

They're easy to spot, because they always follow the same pattern. No matter what I suggest they do, they have ten reasons why it won't work. And no matter how bad their situation, after our meeting they go out and continue doing exactly what got them into the mess in the first place.

What's more, they tend to come back to me again and again, each time asking for more advice—though once they get it, they're guaranteed to blow it off as unreasonable and unworkable.

The first few times this happened, I didn't know how to respond. I wanted to be kind and gracious, so when they'd call and ask for another meeting, I'd go ahead and schedule it. They'd come in, and we'd go through the same drill as before. They'd ask what to do; I'd tell them; then they'd go out and do whatever they wanted to do or had been doing all along.

One young man stands out in particular. His struggle with moral purity must have chalked up thirty to forty hours of my time. Each time we met, I'd tell him the same thing: "Run!"

But instead of running, he continued to hang around the temptation, in this case a woman in his apartment complex with whom he had an ongoing, "friends with benefits," casual sexual relationship.

He claimed he wanted to stop—desperately. But instead of following my advice, he kept trying to overcome the temptation with a new burst of self-discipline, prayer, or extra Bible study. He didn't think the biblical admonitions to flee sexual temptations actually applied to him. He was somehow different.

But, alas, he wasn't.

THE THREE STRIKE RULE

After my frustrating encounters with him, it wasn't long before I instituted what I call a Three Strike Rule. It goes like this: Ask me anything, and I'll give you the best advice I can. Ask me a second time, and I'll do the same, even if you ignored me the first time. Ask a third time, and I'll still give it my best shot. But after that, it's strike three.

And we all know what happens after strike three. "You're out!"

When someone crosses the three-strike threshold, I'm done. I won't waste any more time seeking God's counsel and giving advice that I know won't be followed. It simply makes no sense to keep trying.

> I won't waste time giving advice that I know won't be followed.

Occasionally a three-striker successfully corners me for another round. They'll catch me in a hallway, get my phone number or email, or in some other way beat the system and show up on my schedule.

Whenever that happens, the dialogue invariably goes something like this.

After explaining their situation to me, they'll ask, "What do you think I should I do?"

I'll say, "What do *you* think you should do?"

And no matter how they answer, I'll reply with something like this: "That sounds like *your* plan to me."

I know nothing is going to change their mind. So I'd rather shrug my shoulders and get the meeting over with, knowing they'll go out anyway and do exactly what they planned to do all along.

Amazingly, after some of these three-strike encounters, I've received cards and notes thanking me for my listening ear and helpful advice. It's as if by no longer challenging their plans, I prove myself to be a valuable source of profound wisdom.

Go figure.

THE CONSULTANT GOD

The sad truth is that when it comes to God, we can do the exact same thing these hard-headed counselees do, but with one major difference. When God gives advice or guidance, it's not coming from a potentially fallible source. It's not the mere advice of a pastor or friend; it's the counsel of God!

When God speaks, it doesn't make much sense to push back or give him ten reasons why it won't work. That's an argument we can't win.

But who hasn't done this? We've all had times when we knew exactly what God wanted us to do, but we still decided that in our particular case our own wisdom was better than his.

Every time that happens, our relationship with him goes through a fundamental role-reversal. He stops being our God and becomes our cosmic consultant.

Now, a consultant is someone whose wisdom we highly value and listen to, but at the end of the day, *we* make the final decision. That's why they're called consultants.

Here's the problem: God doesn't do consulting. Never has. Never will. He does *God*. When we treat him as a consultant, he simply stops showing up to the meetings. We may think he's there. But he's not.

THE DIMMER SWITCH PRINCIPLE

And it gets worse. God not only stops showing up to the meetings, he also pulls back some of the light he's already given us.

I call this phenomenon, the Dimmer Switch Principle. It has a profound impact upon our spiritual life for both good and bad. Yet in many circles, it gets scant attention.

Once understood, it explains a great deal: Why spiritual insights seem to come in spurts; why the spigot of God's leading can suddenly run dry; and why some people who once possessed great spiritual insight can regress to the point of mind-boggling folly.

> God doesn't do consulting. Never has. Never will.

It's a simple principle. Here's how it works: When we respond to the light we have, God gives us more. When we don't, he takes away the light we already have.

Now catch this. It's not just that we stop growing when we ignore what we already know. We actually lose the light we once had.

That's the clear implication in Scripture when the apostle Paul, in the first chapter of Romans, describes the downward spiral of a culture that has turned its back on God.[7] Three times in this passage he points out that their increasing moral decay is the direct result of having rejected the truth they already knew. And in each case, God turns them over to even greater depravity and darkness. In other words, he puts his hand on the dimmer switch and turns down the light!

On the other hand, whenever we respond to the light we have—no matter how dim it may be—God grabs the light switch and turns it up.

Note these words in Proverbs:

The path of the righteous is like the first gleam of dawn, shining ever brighter till the full light of day. But the way of the wicked is like deep darkness; they do not know what makes them stumble.[8]

Think back to an early morning experience. At the first gleam of dawn, there's not much to see. Without a full moon or other ambient light, everything looks the same. The reason is that our night vision, like our peripheral vision, lacks color and detail.

I remember camping one summer in Yosemite National Park. I woke up just before dawn and decided to head to the restroom. On my way, I caught the outline of a small boulder. As I walked toward it, I readied myself to use it as a stepping stone.

That was before it moved.

To my surprise, it wasn't a small boulder. It was a small bear cub. As it sauntered over to momma, I shuddered at the thought of what I'd almost done. In the predawn darkness, I'd been unable to tell the difference between a boulder and a bear. I had no idea of the danger in front of me.

If the little guy hadn't moved before I stepped on him, momma and I would have had a rather unpleasant and unplanned encounter.

Yet just ten minutes later, I would have had no problem telling the difference. The first gleam of dawn would have revealed something unique about the texture and shape of the lump in front of me. With a second glance, I would have easily recognized it as a bear. And by the time the sun rose to shed its full light, I'd have been able to distinguish all the different shades of brown in its hide.

At the beginning of our journey with God, many of us don't do a very good job discerning between right and wrong. Sure, we may know and understand a few things—like, if the boulder moves, don't step on it. But all in all, our spiritual discernment has more in common with a night light than a spot light.

But the longer we walk in obedience, the clearer the spiritual picture becomes. Subtle distinctions that were once indiscernible become obvious; things we would have never noticed at first suddenly can't be missed.

I find this to be incredibly encouraging. It means I don't have to worry about all the things I don't know. I just have to respond to the light I have, and the rest will come in God's time.

> God-pleasing spirituality can happen instantly—the moment I start the journey!

It means God-pleasing spirituality can happen instantly—the moment I start the journey!

Maturity and spiritual depth take time. But I can please God right away because it's not a matter of how much I know or how long I've been at it. It's a matter of what I do with what I already have that matters most.

It also means I don't have to dump a truckload of theology and spiritual protocol on every new Christian I have the privilege of introducing to the Lord. All I need to do is help them obey the light they already have, because if they do that, the rest will come quickly enough.

PRIDE AND INTIMIDATION

Rightly understood, the Dimmer Switch Principle undercuts the common assumption that those of us who know the most about the Bible and theology are also the most spiritual.

It counters the spiritual intimidation so many of us feel in the presence of those who are far more theologically astute or biblically literate.

Fact is, any cursory reading of the New Testament reveals that the biblical scholars and theologians of the day were the ones most at odds with Jesus and his message, while the unschooled and the common folks got it.

Yet we see this intimidation all the time. Those of us who don't know all the "right" answers clam up, thinking we don't measure up. Meanwhile those of us who know the right answers puff up, filled with a pride that can be easily detected in our patronizing corrections of those who don't know everything we know.

This is not to say Bible knowledge and theology are unimportant. They are. But they don't equal pleasing God.

In reality, when it comes to spiritual growth, the amount of light we have at any given time isn't nearly as important as what we're *doing* with that light—and whether God is in the process of turning it up or down.

INSIDE OUT

ULTIMATELY, SPIRITUAL GROWTH is an inside-out job. It's not something we produce. It's something God does. Yes, we can cooperate or resist him in the process, but the bulk of the work and *all* the credit goes to him.

At least that's what Jesus said. But the first time he tried to explain it, no one got it. Many still don't.

IT WAS JUST HOURS before his arrest when Jesus and his most trusted followers gathered to share the Passover meal. Jesus knew it would be their last time together before his arrest and crucifixion, so he began to prepare them for the tough days ahead.

He told them many things, none more confusing than his assertion that he was about to leave them—and that leaving them would actually be a good thing for them.

This had to mess with their minds. Only recently they had come to the full realization of who Jesus was. Far more than a great teacher, prophet, and leader, he was the promised Messiah—the great deliverer for whom God's people had waited so long.

Now he was talking about leaving, claiming this would be even better for them than if he stayed. It must have struck them as total nonsense.

But it wasn't nonsense. It was part of the plan. Once he was gone, the Holy Spirit would be sent to come and live within them; while he was around, that couldn't happen.

If only his hearers had understood what he was saying, they would have been awestruck. The promise was breathtaking.

Jesus was telling them that the exact same Spirit who had guided and empowered *his* ministry and life was about to come and provide each of them with all the spiritual guidance, instruction, and power they'd ever need. And he'd do it from the inside out, just like he had with Jesus.

Wow!

Yet, at the time, they hardly grasped a word of it.

VISIONS OF GRANDEUR

With hindsight, it's understandable. Their minds were too filled with dreams of grandeur.

They'd arrived in Jerusalem just a few days earlier, having come to celebrate the Passover as required by Jewish law. Throughout the trip Jesus had been dropping hints that he was up to something big, that this would be an especially eventful visit to the holy city.

To their ears, this could mean only one thing: He was about to reveal himself to the masses. He was about to take over as king.

They were so sure of it, they'd been secretly arguing behind his back about who would have what roles in the royal court. Two of them, James and John, had even gone so far as to have their mother lobby Jesus on their behalf, seeking prime positions for them in the new regime.

With throngs of fellow pilgrims swelling the streets for

Passover, the timing must have seemed perfect. The only problem was the religious leaders. They weren't on board. But surely once Jesus revealed himself and set up his kingdom, they'd come around quickly enough.

The Roman oppressors? They wouldn't have a chance. Not with Jesus leading the way. He'd already shown his mastery over disease, demons, nature, and even death. He'd stilled the storm, walked on water, and raised the dead. Even the world's greatest army couldn't stand up to that kind of power!

His disciples had to be pumped. Everything was falling their way. They'd hooked up with the Messiah and been picked for his inner circle. Now, in just a few days, he would be king, and they'd be set for life.

But as we all know, that's not how it played out.

Jesus didn't conquer the Romans. He didn't set up an earthly kingdom. He was arrested and killed.

And even when he came back to life three days later, it still wasn't to overthrow the Romans or set up an earthly kingdom.

Instead, he spent the days immediately following his resurrection instructing and preparing his followers to lead a heavenly kingdom. And then, without much warning, he left them again—this time floating up into the heavens as they watched helplessly below.

He did promise to come back. They thought and hoped it would be soon. (Two thousand years later, we're still waiting.)

How could this be a good thing?

BETTER WITHOUT JESUS?

A short time later it all made sense to them.

As they waited in the upper room for the promised Spirit, he suddenly showed up. Instantly they experienced what Jesus had promised. The same Spirit who had guided and empowered him for ministry now resided within them. It's an amazing story. (You can find all the details in the second chapter of the book of Acts.)

Up to this point, the only time his followers had been able to experience the full power, guidance, and wisdom of God was when they were in the physical presence of Jesus. Now that limitation was gone.

The Spirit was no longer simply *with* them (in the sense of being present when they were with Jesus). He was *in* them (just as he had been in Jesus).

With that simple but profound change, the hyper-expansion of Christianity began. No longer bound by the limitations of Jesus' physical presence, the gospel's power and message spread at a dizzying pace, accompanied by signs, wonders, and the amazing miracles of conversion and spiritual transformation.

The disciples were no longer relegated to the role of Jesus' entourage, road crew, and set-up team. They were the fully empowered messengers of God.

No wonder Jesus said it would be better when he was gone!

But it wasn't just a good thing for *them*.

It's also a great thing for *us*.

No wonder Jesus said it would be better when he was gone!

That's because the disciples weren't the only ones to receive the Holy Spirit. We receive him too. Paul expressed it this way: "If anyone does not have the Spirit of Christ, he does not belong to Christ."[9]

In other words, if I'm a genuine Christ follower, I have available within me the same Holy Spirit who instructed, guided, and empowered Jesus and the early disciples.

And that means my spiritual growth isn't so much the result of my hard work, intellect, and rigid self-discipline (all of which I could boast about). Instead, it's the direct result of my willingness to listen and yield to the Spirit's inner promptings as he works to guide and change me from the inside out.

STATIC ON THE LINE

But if that's so, why don't we experience the same crystal-clear leading and flow of power that Jesus did? Why does his guidance sometimes seem obscure and his power anemic?

The answer is simple. Unlike Jesus, we all struggle with sin. We're fallen sons and daughters of Adam living in a fallen world. Our thinking and spiritual understanding, even at their best, are marred by the impact of our fallen nature. On top of that, we all make our own intentionally sinful choices and suffer the consequences. All this puts static on the line. It hinders us from hearing clearly the Spirit's leading and restricts the free flow of his power.

It's always been that way. Whether we're trying to discern God's leading at the feet of a physical Jesus in Galilee or through the inner promptings of the Holy Spirit, we've always had and always will have to deal with some static on the line.

To overcome the impact of that static, and to free up the Spirit to do his work, we have a role to play. It's not a matter of digging deep to produce our own spiritual growth. It's more in line with being willing to let go of our own agenda and allowing him the freedom to genuinely change us from the inside out.

YIELDING TO THE SPIRIT

Theologians have often called this concept "yielding to the Spirit." But *yielding* is not a word we use much these days. For most people, it brings up images of an intersection and the need to let the other guy go first.

It's a good word, though, and a great word-picture once we fully grasp it.

In its simplest terms, yielding to the Spirit and letting him change us from the inside out can be broken down into three parts.

FIRST, IT MEANS *removing as much static as possible*. That primarily happens when we obey what we already know. As we saw with the Dimmer Switch Principle, obeying what I know always brings more light—and less static.

But notice I didn't say that it removes *all* the static. That won't happen this side of heaven. No matter how much we try to obey what we know, we will always have more blind spots to be exposed and areas of ongoing struggle to overcome. It's part of the human condition.

Additionally, for many of us there will be areas of spiritual insight we're simply not yet ready for. Spiritual growth is a lot like intellectual growth. There are things a five-year-old can't grasp, no matter how hard he tries—things he can't know no matter how much we wish he could. We too will have areas where the foundational prerequisites for understanding are simply not yet in place. The result: We're left with some static on the line.

THE SECOND COMPONENT of yielding to the Spirit is *openness to the help and insight of other believers*. The Bible calls this seeking wise counsel. It's important, because my areas of static are often another person's area of great clarity.

By checking in with others, I have the ability to pick up what I missed on my own and to discover and correct what I might have misunderstood.

Like most people, I have a telephone answering machine. Most of the time I have no problem understanding the messages. But every now and then someone spouts off a return number or name so quickly I have no clue what they said. Couple that with a weak cell phone signal, and I'm lost.

I've been known to replay a message five or six times. No matter. I still don't have a clue.

But it's amazing what another set of ears can do. Or if the message is really garbled, two or three sets of ears. Each of us picks up something different. Most of the time, by working together, we can decipher the number or name well enough to respond.

The same power of collaboration can bring clarity when God's leading seems unclear or hard to decipher. Of course the problem is not on God's end. He doesn't speak too fast or send a weak signal. The problem is always the static on my end of the line. Nonetheless, seeking the help of others can bring to light things I miss—or even more importantly, things I thought I heard quite clearly but in reality missed quite badly.

THE THIRD COMPONENT of yielding is primarily a heart matter: *Am I willing to let God change me?* Really change me? Not just empower me to do his will, not just show me his will, but actually change—from the inside out—how I feel and what I want.

I've found that in many cases this is the missing piece to spiritual growth. Most Christians understand that God is supposed to provide us with the power to do the right thing, but we've short-changed his promise to also provide us with the desire and motivation to do the right thing.

I still remember the first time the full impact of this hit me. I was memorizing the New Testament book of Philippians in preparation to teach it to a group of college students. When I came to the following passage, I was astonished at what it said: "Continue to work out your salvation with fear and trembling, *for it is God who works in you to will and to act according to his good purpose.*"[10] I'd seen these verses before, but that last phrase hadn't really registered.

The idea that I was supposed to work out the implications of my salvation with fear and trembling came as no surprise. Fear and trembling fit my paradigm of spirituality well. Jesus had saved me; now it was up to me to work it out. It was my job to stay motivated, figure out what God wanted, then suck it up and do the right thing.

But that's not what this passage said. It said God would provide more than just the power. It said he would provide upstream the desire, will, and motivation to carry out his good purpose.

That simple insight rocked my world. It completely changed my approach to spirituality. Before, I had prayed primarily for the power the Spirit provided, and when I didn't want to do what I knew I should, I'd pray, "Lord, help me do it." But now I began to pray, "Lord help me *want* to do it."

And he did!

What a difference that made. The entire process of spiritual growth became much more organic and natural. And with God providing up front the will and desire, aligning my actions with his will became a whole lot easier.

THE PRAYER OF PERMISSION

To my surprise, I found that letting God change my upstream desires wasn't as simple as I thought. It's not that he couldn't do it. It's that, more often than I'd like to admit, I didn't want him to.

I've discovered that this is where many of us short-circuit the inside-out work of the Spirit. We're willing to let God provide us with power, but we don't want him messing with our attitudes, feelings, and desires.

Let me show you what I mean. As an example, let's take bitterness and the need to forgive.

When we've been wronged, most of us are all too happy to let the Spirit hold us back from seeking revenge or launching out in a verbal tirade. But the greater the injustice, the more reluctant we can be to let God step in and change the way we feel about the person we need to forgive.

The Holy Spirit—a brief fly-by:

And I will ask the Father, and he will give you another Counselor to be with you forever—the Spirit of truth. (John 14:16–17)

But the Counselor, the Holy Spirit, whom the Father will send in my name, will teach you all things and will remind you of everything I have said to you. (John 14:26)

[Jesus saying, 'It's better for you that I leave']—But I tell you the truth: It is for your good that I am going away. Unless I go away, the Counselor will not come to you; but if I go, I will send him to you. When he comes, he will convict the world of guilt in regard to sin and righteousness and judgment: in regard to sin, because men do not believe in me; in regard to righteousness, because I am going to the Father, where you can see me no longer; and in regard to judgment, because the prince of this world now stands condemned. I have much more to say to you, more than you can now bear. But when he, the Spirit of truth, comes, he will guide you into all truth. He will not speak on his own; he will speak only what he hears, and he will tell you what is yet to come. He will bring glory to me by taking from what is mine and making it known to you. All that belongs to the Father is mine. That is why I said the Spirit will take from what is mine and make it known to you (John 16:7–15)

It's as if we're afraid that a full removal of our feelings of anger or bitterness somehow lets the perpetrator off the hook. So we try to do the actions of forgiveness while holding onto the feelings of hostility.

As we all know, that doesn't work too well.

A big part of the problem is that many of us were taught that one of the greatest signs of spiritual maturity is the self-discipline to do God's will even when we don't want to. We don't see it as a problem when our desires fail to align with his; it's just another opportunity to prove our spiritual worth.

But if the Spirit's job is to provide us with both the will and the power to do God's good purposes, then any time my desire fails to match up with his, it doesn't just call for self-disciplined obedience. It calls for a spiritual realignment.

When I find myself knowing what to do but not wanting to do it, I'm no longer satisfied to obey with some sort of macho self-denial and hard obedience. If that's all I've got, God hasn't changed me much.

Instead, I take that as a sign that I need to go back to the heart of the matter—to give him permission to realign my desires with his, and to let the Spirit genuinely change me from the inside out.

At this point, I often pray what I've come to call the Prayer of Permission. It goes something like this: "Lord, I know what you want me to do, but I don't want to do it. I'm giving you full permission to change the way I feel and think about it."

It's my way of admitting to God that I don't want what he wants, and of humbly facing the fact that the real reason for this is my failure to yield to his leading on the matter.

A BETTER (AND EASIER) WAY

Like a disciplined child forced to sit in the corner—whose last vestige of self-determination is found in defiantly thinking, "Yeah, but I'm still standing on the inside!"—I've too often tried to obey on the outside while disobeying on the inside. My bet is, you have too.

The result is always the same. It makes doing the right thing way tougher than it ought to be, and it brings the inside-out work of the Spirit to a screeching halt.

Contrary to what so many of us have been led to believe with sermon illustrations and Sunday school stories, the greatest sign of God's work in our life is not a pattern of rugged self-denial and dig-deep obedience. It's *wanting what God wants*—then going out and doing it.

Like Jesus in Gethsemane, we may face a struggle to get there at times. But ultimately, if we'll honestly give the Spirit permission to do his inside-out work, he'll align our will with his.

I find this to be extraordinarily encouraging. If spiritual growth wasn't an inside-out job, only the few, the strong, and the mighty would have a chance. But thanks to the gift of the Spirit, there's hope for the rest of us.

PART

3

WHAT DOES GOD WANT?

CHAPTER NINE

THE HIGH PLACE PRINCIPLE

Blind Spots—Yours, Mine, and Theirs

SO WHAT DOES GOD WANT from us? We've seen what genuine spirituality looks like, and we've explored how we grow. But what kind of spiritual expressions actually spur God's delight and bring his blessings? And what kind of things leave him cold?

In my early days as a Christian, I thought the answers to these questions were obvious. That's because my small circle of Christian friends and spiritual mentors walked in lock-step agreement. They had no doubt as to what God wanted, who he blessed—and seemingly most important, who ticked him off.

Since my friends had been at this God thing a lot longer than I had, who was I to argue?

I must admit there was something comforting in our certainty. It made it easy to tell the difference between spiritual friend and foe. All I had to do was pull out my little checklist to see how you measured up.

It provided me with a clearly marked path for pleasing God. As long as I held firmly to all our theological distinctives and toed the line on our list of do's and don'ts, God would be happy, and I'd have a great shot at being blessed and used by him.

But the more I read the Bible rather than just listening to their sermons and Bible studies, the more it chipped away at my certitude. My nice little boxes of who's in and who's out didn't fit too well with what I was reading.

The biblical stories were unequivocal. God often liked to hang with and bless the very people I'd been told he'd want nothing to do with.

I'm not talking here about vile and wicked folks who hate God and stridently pursue a godless agenda (though I recall Jesus saying they were the very people he'd come to seek and to save).

I'm talking about self-identified God-followers who don't play by all our rules, don't know all our rules, or otherwise fail to measure up to the high standards of what we've always been told a friend of God should look like.

There was no getting around it. Whether it was a chronic deceiver like Jacob, a horn-dog like Samson, a never-believe-God-the-first-time warrior like Gideon, or a zealous persecutor like the apostle Paul, God had a way of blessing and using the wrong people.

At first this left me troubled. If God's grace was so great that he didn't care how we lived, why bother to clean up my own act? Why spend time and energy seeking out spiritual truth? Why worry about upholding his standards if he didn't care?

BLIND SPOTS

Then one day it hit me. It's not that God doesn't have high standards. His standards are incredibly high. But he understands and makes allowances for something most of us leave out of the spiritual equation—spiritual blind spots.

Blind spots don't get a lot of play in Christian circles. It's not that we're unaware of them. We all know they're there. But we don't know what to do with them.

That's because a blind spot in someone else doesn't look like a blind spot. It looks like high-handed disobedience. Anything we see clearly, we have a hard time believing others can't see just as clearly. When they miss it on a lifestyle issue, we see it as blatant sin. If it's a theological issue, we chalk it up to a hardened heart resisting the truth.

As for our own blind spots, by definition we don't know where they are. So when God

> God understands and makes allowances for spiritual blind spots.

shows us his favor, it hardly strikes us as odd or especially gracious. We think it's what we deserve. After all, we measure up pretty well in comparison to those whose inconsistencies and shortcomings we think we see clearly.

This is not to confuse high-handed sin with a blind spot. A personal choice to rewrite the Bible or to ignore the commands we find uncomfortable is not a blind spot; it's a sin—the willful disobedience that always brings grave consequences.

In contrast, a genuine blind spot is something I honestly don't see. It's a truth I'm literally unable to grasp or an issue I've not yet faced or come to grips with.

New Christians usually are not surprised that God would somehow make allowances for, and sometimes overlook, a blind spot. This idea fits right in with how most of our culture views spiritual truth—the widely believed lie that God is good with anything as long as it's sincerely believed.

But for many longtime Christians—those of us who hold to the concept of absolute truth, and take Jesus at his words, and believe he's the only way to the Father—the idea that God makes allowances for some sins or shortcomings can be hard to swallow. Especially when it's a sin or shortcoming we have no trouble seeing clearly.

In fact, I've noticed that the more theologically astute and spiritually self-disciplined we become, the more likely we are to struggle with, and in many cases explain away, God's propensity to bless and use the wrong people.

I know.

I was once there.

If another Christian saw one of my key doctrines differently than I did, or battled with a sin I'd long ago left behind, or missed badly in obeying a clear exhortation of Scripture, I was sure there was no way God could be pleased with this person.

If the evidence suggested differently—if God actually showed up and blessed and clearly used them—I'd still write them off. After all, if God used Balaam's ass for his purposes, why couldn't he use a modern-day donkey?

The problem was, the more I read the accounts of Jesus' wide circle of acceptance—the people he hung out with and blessed— the more I began to wonder if perhaps I was the one who was missing something.

Then one day I came across an Old Testament story that turned the lights on. It opened my eyes to what I've come to call the High Place Principle. For the first time, the lens God uses when he looks at our efforts to please him came into focus for me.

It's a story I'd read and heard many times before, but each and every time I'd missed the main point. See if you haven't as well.

SOLOMON'S BIG DAY

It's found in the third chapter of 1 Kings. A young King Solomon has gone to Gibeon to make a ceremonial sacrifice to the Lord. That night, in a dream, God comes and offers him anything he wishes. It's an amazing story that brings to mind the mythical accounts of magic genies offering lucky treasure hunters the three wishes of their choice. Only this story really happened.

Rather than asking for riches or the destruction of his enemies, Solomon humbly asked for wisdom to lead God's people. His request so pleased God that he also granted Solomon the riches and honor he didn't ask for.

This story is a Sunday school favorite. Kids hear it from a young age, and long-time church members usually know it well. The emphasis is always the same—Solomon's wise and unselfish choice.

Unfortunately, that's not the story's main point. It's an important point. But not the primary lesson the writer had in mind.

While Solomon's unselfish request for wisdom gives us significant insight into his heart and brings him a great reward, the greater and more widely applicable lesson is found in the first five verses—four of which we usually ignore or skim over in the rush to get to Solomon's response.

In these first four verses of the chapter, we discover critical details about the kind of king Solomon was prior to God's incredible offer—and by implication, the kind of person God meets, blesses, and uses.

The first thing we're told is that Solomon had previously made an alliance with Pharaoh, king of Egypt, and had married Pharaoh's daughter. At first, that seems an odd thing to point out. Egypt has nothing to do with the rest of the story. But it's not a throw-away point. It's key.

By marrying Pharaoh's daughter, Solomon had bought off a major military threat. A huge dowry and the bond of marriage guaranteed peace between the nations.

But such alliances were frowned upon by the Jewish prophets. Centuries later, Isaiah would record this declaration from the Lord:

Woe to the obstinate children...to those who carry out plans that are not mine, forming an alliance, but not by my Spirit, heaping sin upon sin; who go down to Egypt without consulting me; who look for help to Pharaoh's protection, to Egypt's shade for refuge. But Pharaoh's protection will be to your shame, Egypt's shade will bring you disgrace.[11]

The next thing we learn about Solomon is that he allowed the people to continue offering sacrifices at "the high places."

This too was not a good thing. God had specifically told the Israelites, "Drive out all the inhabitants of the land before you. Destroy all their carved images and their cast idols, and *demolish all their high places.*"[12]

These high places were literally high points in the hills that the pagan nations assumed to be closer to God. Yet despite God's clear prohibition, the Israelites not only adopted the same practice, they co-opted the sites.

Their excuse was that a temple had not yet been built. But God hadn't told them they could use the high places until a temple was built; he told them to demolish the high places.

Solomon, however, not only allowed the people to continue sacrificing at these high places; he joined them. Even worse, when it came time to offer a special sacrifice consisting of a thousand burnt offerings to the Lord, Solomon chose to do it on the altar at Gibeon because it was the most famous and important of all the high places.

Even though I was once a blasphemer and a persecutor and a violent man, I was shown mercy because I acted in ignorance and unbelief. (1 Timothy 1:13)

THE HIGH PLACE PRINCIPLE

Now, if I didn't know better, I'd expect the next verse to say, "And God struck dead the evil and disobedient king."

It's bad enough that Solomon refused to tear down the high places. But to mock God with an enormous ceremonial sacrifice on the most famous and important high place; to claim you're showing love and devotion to God at the same time you're ignoring one of his clear commands; that takes real nerve.

Imagine for a moment that you and I could somehow be transported back in time, knowing what we know now and what Solomon should have known all along.

I wonder how many of us would have gathered at Gibeon's altar to protest the king's spiritual compromise and the deteriorating state of the kingdom. How many of us would have plastered a "No High Places" bumper sticker on our chariots? How many emails, broadcasts, and fund-raising letters would have decried his callous spiritual condition and the certain demise of the nation?

But obviously, that's not how God saw it. While some of us would have been warning everyone to stay away, God showed up in a dream and asked Solomon, "What can I do for you?"

There can be only one explanation. Solomon's alliance with Egypt, his marriage to Pharaoh's daughter, and his use of the high places must have been spiritual and cultural blind spots for him and for many of the kings who followed.

How else to explain not only God's response to Solomon, but also the recurring statements in Scripture about other kings who, as we read repeatedly, "did what was right in the eyes of the LORD," but whose commendation is followed immediately by the comment, "The high places, however, were not removed"?[13]

How could they have done right in the eyes of the Lord if they didn't obey what he said?

Yet there's no way around it. That was God's assessment. *His* Scriptures tell us these men did right in the eyes of the Lord.

Of one king, named Asa, the Bible even goes so far as to say, "Although he did not remove the high places, Asa's heart was fully committed to the LORD all his life."[14]

Fully committed to the Lord?

All his life?

> We all have our own areas where we simply don't get it.

Again, how can that be—if God said to destroy the high places, and Asa didn't? Most of us would hardly call this guy "fully committed."

But God did.

The fact is, we all have our own high places—areas where we simply don't get it. While I can't fathom how Solomon and future kings missed it in regard to sacrificing on pagan high places, it's really no different from Martin Luther's virulent anti-Semitic statements, or American Christians who supported racial slavery or who accepted segregation.

All are profoundly disturbing with our 20/20 hindsight.

Yet in each case, God met and used these people despite their high places.

ALTERED PERCEPTIONS

Coming to grips with this High Place Principle radically altered my perception of what God wants from both me and others.

It's made me much slower to assail those who appear to be following Jesus but who hold viewpoints or positions that strike me as wrongheaded or out of line with Scripture.

And while I won't hesitate to point out sin or anything that digresses from Scripture, I'm now far more willing to say my piece and then back off, having learned that the situation might be a "high place" rather than high-handed disobedience or a hardened heart, as I'd always assumed.

I also no longer explain it away when God blesses or uses someone who's too far to the left or right on some issue which I see as critical and even biblically clear. Same goes for those mired in the wishy-washy middle. Could be it's their blind spot.

Heaven forbid, it could even be mine.

I've also found it's a lot easier to follow Jesus' command to deal with the speck in my eye when I recognize that the log in someone else's eye might not be the sin or spiritual insensitivity I'm so quick to label it.

In fact, a good grasp of this High Place Principle has proved to be the perfect antidote for log-eye disease, the all too common spiritual ailment that often afflicts those of us who take our walk with God seriously.

BACK TO SIMPLICITY

God's decision to bless Solomon despite his high-place sacrifices has also helped me to be less uptight in regard to my own spiritual journey.

Once I grasp that God understands and makes allowances for my own high places, there's no longer a reason to lie awake at night worrying if I've somehow unintentionally missed it on a critical issue or area of obedience.

While I'm still responsible to align my thoughts and actions with Scripture whenever a high place or blind spot is brought to light and understood, I no longer have the unfounded and unbiblical fear of a God in heaven ready to pounce in judgment at the first sign of an innocent misstep or a failure to grasp what he wants.

Instead, Solomon's story brings me back to the simplicity of the Dimmer Switch Principle. As long as I obey the light I have, I can be spiritually confident. As long as I continue to respond to any new light he gives, I'll be on the right track—even if I've got a high place or two that you can see all too clearly. As long as I can't see it, or haven't yet seen it, God and I can still be on the best of terms.

So what does God want from us? Bottom line: It's the same thing he's always wanted, whether in Old Testament days or now. He wants obedience to the light we have. That has always been and always will be the shortest path to God-pleasing spirituality—whether we're a king in Jerusalem or a cobbler in Corinth.

CHAPTER TEN

THE MUSTARD SEED PRINCIPLE

Is Faith Overrated?

WHEN IT COMES to God-pleasing spirituality, faith is undeniably a big deal. We're constantly told we need more of it.

But as a young Christian, whenever I tried to get my hands around what it was supposed to look, feel, or act like, everything got muddy. It was as if everyone I asked had their own proprietary definition.

At one extreme, the doctrine crowd told me that God-pleasing faith was found primarily in believing the right facts about Jesus and God.

At the other end of the spectrum, the positive thinkers stressed the need for unbridled optimism and fighting off any vestiges of negativity or doubt.

In between, there were countless other iterations and nuanced definitions, each claiming to hold the key to pleasing God and plugging into his power.

Frankly, I was baffled. I had no idea which definition of faith to pursue. But one thing was crystal clear. No matter which camp had the upper hand on a given day, they all shared one message: Whatever faith was, I needed *more* of it—lots more.

That's because faith was usually presented as a tangible object, a concrete thing, something I could choose to have in greater or lesser quantity. The more of it I had, the more I'd please God. The less I had, the less of his help and power I'd have available.

In addition, most of their definitions seemed to imply that faith was engaged in a zero-sum game with its great nemesis— doubt. Apparently the two could not coexist. If one increased, the other, by necessity, decreased. Thus the key to greater faith was pretty straightforward: Eradicate my doubts.

So I tried.

When troubled by qualms about a doctrine, a passage of Scripture, or conventional Christian thinking, I did my best to bury it.

When faced with a trial or the need for God's help and guidance, I sought to cast out all negative thoughts and dwell on the positive.

But the results were less than satisfying. This kind of faith seemed more about putting my mind in neutral or inhabiting the land of happy talk than anything else.

The more I tried to bury my questions, the larger they loomed. The more I tried to think positively, the more negativity crept in— all, of course, in the name of being "realistic."

I marveled at the stories of those who seemed to live above doubt. When they prayed for rain, they carried an umbrella. When they had no money to pay tuition, they signed up for another semester anyway, confident God would come through.

When I prayed for rain, I checked the weather report. If it said hot and dry, I'd put off my prayers until the next day. No need to make God look bad.

DOES GOD WANT ME STUPID?

I remember attending a large rally of so-called Jesus People, many of whom had recently turned from drugs, free sex, and anarchy to follow Christ.

A paunchy, middle-aged pastor stood at the front of the room with Bible in hand. He spoke with hardly a trace of emotion, but with incredible authority. We hung on every word.

That night, his topic was faith and prayer. To drive home the importance of praying with faith, he told us about an experience he'd had a couple of months prior.

Apparently he was driving to a meeting when his car suddenly stalled. Being mechanically inclined, he got out and opened the hood to see what was wrong. It was just as he thought. The alternator had gone bad, and the battery had died.

Bummed about missing the meeting, he went back to tell his passenger they'd have to call a tow truck. But the young man (a new convert) would have none of it.

"Can't we ask God to fix it?"

"Course we can. But the alternator's broken."

"So? Let's pray."

With that, the young man got out of the car, laid his hands on the hood, and turned to the pastor and asked him to pray.

Reluctantly, he did so.

Then the new convert asked the pastor to try starting the car again to see if, perhaps, God had answered their prayers.

Feeling trapped and a bit foolish (after all, he already knew the car couldn't start), the pastor-mechanic gave the ignition a quick turn.

You guessed it. The car started. At least that's how he told the story. They drove on to the meeting without a problem.

As he finished, the application seemed clear to me. Sometimes we can know too much. In this case, his knowledge of auto mechanics made it impossible for him to have enough "faith" to trust God to fix the car. But his mechanically naive young friend had no such disadvantage, so he was able to muster up enough faith to see God answer his prayers.

I remember wondering: Does that mean God wants me stupid? Does growing in faith mean shrinking in knowledge? Or worse, ignoring facts I already know?

I also remember thinking, Is this guy a liar? If God fixes alternators to get pastors to meetings on time, why can't he do a little better with cancer, war, and all the starving kids in Bangladesh?

SO WHAT IS FAITH?

Not long afterward, I began to pursue my own study to see what the Bible actually said about this thing called faith.

Is it really a commodity I can increase or decrease? Is it measured by how much I believe something, or is it measured by what I do? Are faith and doubt opposites, like light and darkness? Or can they co-exist?

The more I explored the biblical accounts and the less I listened to the motivational talks, the more I became convinced that the kind of faith God wanted from me was quite different from the kind I was constantly being exhorted to have.

Bottom line: God wants us to trust him—to trust him enough to do what he says, no matter how we feel or how certain we are that things will work out.

The Greek word translated as "faith" in our Bibles has nothing to do with a powerful imagination, eradicating doubt, or any other form of mind over matter. It has nothing to do with feelings or mental imagery. It has to do with *obedience*.

EVEN IF GOD DOESN'T

The great biblical stories of faith confirm this understanding. They often tell of amazing acts of obedience and power taking place in the lives of people who are literally shocked when God comes through—leaving us with biblical heroes who are hardly the paragons of optimism and positive thinking they're supposed to be.

Take for instance the famous Sunday school story of Shadrach, Meshach, and Abednego found in chapter three of the book of Daniel.

Ordered by King Nebuchadnezzar to bow down and worship a golden idol, they refuse. This so angers the egomaniac king that he threatens to toss them into a fiery furnace. Given another chance, they still refuse to dishonor God.

A furious Nebuchadnezzar then has them tossed into the fire. But instead of being incinerated, they're met by an angel and miraculously preserved. While the king watches in amazement, they walk around unharmed in the middle of the furnace.

Freaked, the king immediately orders them to come out. When they do, he releases them, repents, and worships the true God.

It's a classic Sunday school story of courage, commitment, and God coming through in the clutch. Kids walk out motivated to do the right thing, trusting God to deliver them no matter what.

And without faith it is impossible to please God, because anyone who comes to him must believe that he exists and that he rewards those who earnestly seek him. (Hebrews 11:6)

In the minds of most Christians, Shadrach, Meshach, and Abednego are forever enshrined in the Flannelgraph Hall of Fame as heroes of the faith. Their courageous confidence that God would deliver them is astonishing.

Listen to their bold words:

> O Nebuchadnezzar, we do not need to defend ourselves before you in this matter. If we're thrown into the blazing furnace, the God we serve is able to save us from it, and he will rescue us from your hand, O king.[15]

Wow! Now that's faith! The kind I'd always heard I needed more of. Faced with the option of death or disobedience, they chose neither. Instead they chose obedience, in full confidence that God would deliver them from the king's wrath.

At least that's what you'd think until reading the next verse. Suddenly their bold words about God rescuing them are cast in a different light. Notice the caveat:

> *But even if he does not,* we want you to know, O king, that we will not serve your gods or worship the image of gold you have set up.[16]

"Even if he *does not*"?

What kind of faith is that?

Actually, it's faith at its greatest—trusting God enough to obey, even when we're sure it won't work out in the short run.

These three men had no idea what was about to happen. No one before and no one since has been spared from the fire. They must have been as shocked at their deliverance as King Nebuchadnezzar was. I'd be surprised if their first response wasn't, "Oh no, we've gone to the wrong place!"

The important lesson in this story is not the Sunday school take-home that if we trust God enough and do the right thing, he'll get us out of every fiery jam. While it's certainly true that sometimes God honors our faith and obedience with miraculous deliverance, most often his reward comes much later—in a place and time called eternity.

> Most often God's reward comes much later—in a place and time called eternity.

The important lesson is that God is pleased with obedience, even when we expect the worst.

PETER'S PRAYER MEETING

The New Testament contains an even clearer rebuttal to this idea that God-pleasing faith lives in a doubt-free zone. It's found in Acts chapter twelve.

The story starts with the sad news that King Herod has decapitated the apostle James. He's also arrested the apostle Peter, planning to bring him to public trial and the same fate.

The entire church gathers to pray, desperately pleading with God to spare Peter's life. It's a safe bet Peter is praying the same thing.

Finally, on the eve of his trial, an angel shows up in his prison cell. He awakens Peter, who's fast asleep, chained between two Roman soldiers. As the chains fall off, the angel tells Peter to get dressed, then leads him out as prison doors miraculously open.

Now here's the interesting thing: If praying with faith means imagining whatever we pray for is already a done deal, Peter fails miserably.

When the angel awakens him, he doesn't jump up and shout, "I knew you were coming!"

No, he assumes it's a wild dream or vision.

Not until he's standing in the middle of the street as a free man does it dawn on him that God had actually answered his prayers.

But this story of powerfully answered prayer gets even stranger.

Realizing he's free, Peter immediately heads for the house where everyone is gathered to pray for his release. He knocks on the door and tells a servant girl that it's indeed him. God has answered their prayers.

But she's so excited she forgets to let him in. Instead, she hurries to tell everyone in the prayer meeting the good news.

Their response is telling. No one leaps for joy. No high fives, no hallelujahs, no "Thank you Jesus!"

Instead they rebuke the servant for her naiveté. "Look, he's in a Roman prison. You don't just walk out of a Roman prison. It must be his angel. We need to keep praying."

Meanwhile, Peter stands on the porch pounding on the door. When someone finally comes and lets him in, one word is used to describe the group's response: astonishment.

Not joy. Not praise that God had come through as promised. Not even an isolated "I told you so!"

Just astonishment.

DON'T MISS THIS. Peter and his prayer-meeting friends seem to have had absolutely no expectation that God would really answer their prayers. Their doubts were so great that when God did answer, they didn't believe it.

They had exactly the kind of faith that many of us have been told God won't honor. But he did.

Their faith and trust in God wasn't shown in a buoyant confidence that God would come through. It was shown in the trusting act of obedience—gathering to pray even though they were sure it was a lost cause.

The key lesson here is not that doubt-free faith and prayer can bring great results. It's that God can come through even when we doubt his ability to do so.

Our requirement is to step out in faith and do the right thing, whether it's refusing to worship an idol, gathering for prayer despite the cause being lost, or any other act of obedience. That's what God wants, and that's what pleases him. After that, it's up to him what happens next.

HOW MUCH FAITH DO WE NEED?

So the idea that faith and doubt can't co-exist is questionable. So is the assertion that whatever faith is, we need more of it.

There's a New Testament story that seems to imply the exact opposite—that what we really need is to act upon the faith we already have, no matter how small it might be.

Perhaps you're familiar with Jesus' famous statements about faith the size of a mustard seed being capable of incredible feats, from moving mountains to uprooting mulberry trees and casting them into the sea.

Like most people, I stopped in my tracks the first time I read it. Did Jesus really mean it? Was this literally possible? Or was it hyperbole meant to prove a point? And if so, what was the point?

These mountain-moving passages were presented as a challenge to increase my faith to the level where I could at least move the metaphorical mountains and mulberry trees in my life.

But a closer examination of Jesus' words and the story preceding them shows that he wasn't encouraging us to have "more" faith. He was telling us we already have enough.

See if you don't agree.

We pick up the story in Luke chapter seventeen. Jesus is

instructing his disciples in the ways of his kingdom when he comes to our need for a higher standard of forgiveness.

He tells them,

> So watch yourselves. If your brother sins, rebuke him, and if he repents, forgive him. If he sins against you seven times in a day, and seven times comes back to you and says, "I repent," forgive him. [17]

To his listeners, this kind of forgiveness seemed impossible. The standard was too high. So they responded by telling Jesus, "Increase our faith!" Apparently they assumed that with just a little more faith, they could do this incredibly difficult thing Jesus was asking them to do.

Jesus told them they had it all wrong. He pointed out that with just a mustard seed of faith they could pick up a tree and cast it into the sea. Now a mustard seed was the smallest seed they knew. It represented something tiny, a colloquial phrase for the smallest of small. His point was clear: If a mustard-seed-sized faith could pick up a tree and move it, forgiving seven times a day should be no big deal.

They didn't need more faith. They just needed *to forgive*.

They didn't need to wait until they were pumped up and convinced it would work. They didn't need to muster up visions of God's power and grandeur. They just needed to act upon the tiny bit of faith they had and do what God said: Forgive, even if it seems like a losing proposition.

That's the kind of faith God wants.

He wants faith that acts and obeys, even when it's riddled with doubts.

Contrary to what many of us have been taught, it's not the

amount of faith that matters. What brings God's favor and power is our willingness to obey and act upon whatever tiny bit of faith we have.

JUST GET ON THE PLANE

I fly a lot. Like most road warriors, I get on a plane with complete confidence I'll arrive safely at my destination. Crashing never enters my mind. My faith and confidence in the airline is exemplary—at least, according to the way many of my Christian friends would define faith. I have no doubts, and I have lots of confidence.

Occasionally I'll see someone get on the plane who's obviously scared to death. Forced to fly against their better judgment by a death in the family or some other time-sensitive crisis, they take their seat with plenty of uncertainty as to whether this thing will fly.

You can see the fear in their eyes. They panic when the landing gear folds in with a loud thump. They're terrified at the first sign of turbulence. Their faith and confidence in the airline is shamefully nonexistent—at least, as many of my Christian friends would define faith.

Yet as long as they get on the plane, wherever the plane goes, they'll go. As long as the plane is airworthy, all their doubt, fear, and terror won't keep them from arriving safely. And conversely, if the plane is doomed, all my trust and confidence in airline safety won't keep me from plowing into the ground.

The same thing goes for our faith in God. It's not how much or little we have that matters. It's whether we're willing to act upon the mustard seed we've got and to get on the plane—doing what he commands even if we're pretty sure it won't work.

CHAPTER ELEVEN

WHAT'S ZEAL GOT TO DO WITH IT?

First Love Lost

As a new Christian I was pumped. Every chance I got, I'd tell people about Jesus. I couldn't get enough Bible study. Worship was an emotional high. It was like being infatuated with God. In my newfound faith, I wanted to know and experience everything I could.

It all seemed so natural. It certainly wasn't something I chose. I did nothing to fan the flame. It burned red hot on its own.

I remember hearing a few sermons about that time on the need to maintain or restore a passionate fervor for God. Frankly, they made little sense to me. I assumed I'd always be fired up about God. To my thinking, anyone who needed to be prodded to restore their lost zeal for God probably never had it in the first place.

Obviously I didn't understand how real relationships work. I was young and single. I didn't realize that all relationships go through predictable stages; that seasons, as well as natural ebbs and flows, are unavoidable—even in a relationship with God.

FIRST LOVE

Looking back, I was like a teenager in the grips of first love. It never dawned on me that my initial intensity could, over time, be replaced with something better or deeper or stronger.

So when my early enthusiasm began to wane, I thought something was terribly wrong. Suddenly I was fair game for all the get-right-with-God sermons and exhortations I'd once blown off as unnecessary for a real Christian.

Every time I'd hear one, I'd repent and try to go back. I'd do my best to reproduce the zeal and intensity of those early days. But it never seemed to work for long—a day or two at most.

All this left me feeling like a spiritual fraud, as if I'd somehow let God down.

It shouldn't have. Looking back, I understand now why I couldn't will myself to once again experience the emotions I'd had at first. Emotions don't work that way. They can't be fabricated, no matter how hard we try.

Relationships don't work that way either, whether it's a relationship with a friend, a spouse, or God himself.

Imagine if my wife Nancy and I judged the quality of our marriage based on our ability to maintain all the initial emotions of our first few months dating. No matter how hard we might try, we can never duplicate the wonder of those first late-night, bare-our-soul conversations, or the rush of the first time we held hands, or the exhilaration of a first kiss.

We've moved on.

But that doesn't mean we've lost something. On the contrary, we've added a magnificent depth and fullness to our relationship that makes the exciting but shallow whitewater experiences of those early days pale in comparison.

The same goes for a relationship with God. It makes no sense to judge its quality by how well we're able to maintain the excitement of the first few months of newfound faith. If it's a real and personal relationship, it will mature and change over time. The initial zeal and wonder will run its course, hopefully to be augmented by a deeper level of devotion and commitment.

> With the passage of time, passion and zeal tend to be experienced quite differently than they were at first.

That's not to say passion and zeal are unimportant. They're very important. But with the passage of time, they tend to be experienced quite differently than they were at the beginning.

A FLY IN THE OINTMENT

All this is well and good, except for one thing. There's a passage of Scripture that seems to blow apart everything I just said.

It's found in Revelation chapter two, in the first seven verses. Here Jesus offers a stinging rebuke to a once-great church located in the city of Ephesus. This church has fallen to such depths that Jesus threatens to remove his presence if things don't turn around.

Their big sin? Here's what Jesus said: "I hold this against you: You have forsaken your first love."

His solution? "Repent and do the things you did at first" (in other words, "Get back to your first love")—or he would be gone.[18]

Yikes! Does that mean our relationship with God is somehow different than all other relationships? Does God expect us to maintain for the long haul the fever pitch of our earliest days, even though it's impossible in every other relationship?

On the surface, it sure seems so.

This passage more than any other has fostered the idea that God-pleasing spirituality flows out of red-hot passion and zeal for the Lord and his agenda.

It's so famous and well known that most Christians (and most Bible teachers) accept without question the prevailing view that it portrays a Lord who's hurt and angry because he's no longer their priority number one. It's the ultimate *You've Lost That Lovin' Feeling* passage (if you're old enough to remember the Righteous Brothers—or young enough to have listened to the many covers of their songs).

And this isn't the only portion of Scripture that seems to imply we need to maintain a high level of spiritual zeal and passion. So do the psalms of David. Every time I read them, I'm awed and convicted by his obvious fervor and zeal for God. I wonder if he represents the norm—the kind of emotions and intensity God wants from all of us, all the time.

My more emotive and mystical friends sure think so. They easily identify with David's strong emotions—both the highs and the lows. For many of them, his psalms are their favorite Scriptures.

I also have to contend with the words of Jesus, especially his teaching that the first and greatest commandment is fulfilled by loving the Lord our God with all our heart, soul, and mind. Like Revelation 2 and David's psalms, this too seems to point to zeal and passion as being essential ingredients to God-pleasing spirituality.

SECOND THOUGHTS

But the longer I walk with God and the more I study these passages, the more I've come to question the standard interpretations.

Take David's psalms for example. Certainly he was an extraordinary man, greatly used by God and loved by God. But his psalms are more a description of one man's faith journey than a prescription of what God wants from all of us.

David is an awesome example of God's grace. But for his every spiritual success, he had an equal or greater failure. I don't think any of us would want to literally follow in his footsteps.

I know his passion and zeal are usually chalked up as a sign of deep spirituality. But I'm not so sure why. They strike me more as a reflection of David's personality than anything else. This was a man who was passionate about everything—passionate enough to be called a man after God's own heart, but also passionate in his pursuit of a friend's wife. It's hardly a pattern I'd want to model my own spiritual journey after.

AS FOR JESUS' CALL for us to love the Lord our God with all our heart, soul, and mind, I'm afraid this too has often been misunderstood. Jesus isn't asking for greater fervor and emotional zeal in this passage. He's exhorting us to keep God always at the center of everything in our lives.

A major reason for our confusion on this issue can be found in the different ways the English and Greek languages use the words *love* and *heart*.

In English, the word *love* carries a strong emotional component. When we hear Jesus telling us to love God, we tend to read into it a good amount of feelings and emotions. But the New Testament was originally written in Greek, and the Greek word translated as "love" doesn't necessarily convey anything about feelings or emotions. It conveys self-sacrifice and putting others first.

A similar thing happens with the word translated as "heart." The English and Greek languages use this word quite differently. In English, we think of the heart as the seat of our emotions. When we hear we're supposed to love God with all our heart, we think of intense emotion.

But to those who spoke the language of the New Testament, the heart was not the seat of emotion; it was the seat of the will. (They saw the stomach as the seat of their emotions.) A command to love God with all their heart would have been interpreted not in terms of feelings, but in terms of a deep-rooted act of the will, a profound and unchangeable dedication and commitment to the things of God.

WHAT'S ZEAL GOT TO DO WITH IT?

The biggest change in my thinking about this has come as a result of reexamining Jesus' rebuke to the Ephesian church in Revelation 2.

The passage was so familiar, I thought I knew it well. But one day, while preparing to teach it to a Bible study group, I realized for the first time that it didn't say what I'd always thought it said. My familiarity had blinded me to the main point.

I'd always thought of the Ephesian church as going through the motions—playing church, if you will. To my mind, they were hard working and did lots of religious things, but they'd lost sight of their original feelings of passion and zeal for God. That was why Jesus rebuked them for having forsaken their first love.

But when I read the passage carefully, a different picture emerged. In actuality, the first four verses of Revelation 2 describe a church incredibly zealous and passionate for God. Their deeds were noteworthy, their dedication exemplarily. Their determination in the face of all obstacles was remarkable. Jesus said so himself.

On top of that, they didn't wink at sin, but dealt with it swiftly. They also took doctrine seriously; they had no room for false teaching. And when things got tough, they dug in and hung on.

This description hardly sounds like a church that's lost its passion and zeal for God. Put a church like that in today's world, and people would be flying in from all around the country to packed-out conferences, seeking to learn how they do it and what it takes to follow in their footsteps.

This was one on-fire congregation. They hadn't grown cold or apathetic; they were *not* just playing church.

But they did have a big problem, and the Lord was angry about it—angry enough that he threatened to pick up and leave if they didn't fix it soon.

They'd forsaken their first love. It was no longer anywhere to be found.

A DIFFERENT KIND OF LOVE

To understand what Jesus meant by *first love,* we need to freeze-frame this passage for a moment and jump over to another famous portion of Scripture, the so-called love chapter found in 1 Corinthians 13.

Even the newest or most marginal follower of Jesus usually has some acquaintance with this passage and its definition of love. It's quoted or sung at countless weddings. It's often referred to in sermons on marriage, the family, sharing our faith, getting along with others, dealing with our enemies, and a host of other topics.

It's here that we find the biblical definition of a special kind of love—*agape* love.

Agape was a rarely used Greek word for love that was picked up and used by the early Christians to describe the sacrificial kind of love God has for us, and the kind we're supposed to have for others.

By this all men will know that you are my disciples, if you love one another." (John 13:35)

And virtually every time someone speaks on this text, one of the main things they point out is that *agape* love is not a feeling, but an action. It's a love that puts the needs and interests of others first, whether we feel like it or not. In fact, the entire list of attributes used to define *agape* love in verses four through eight in 1 Corinthians 13 is made up of action words. Not one refers to feelings or emotion.

This famous passage on love not only emphasizes that *agape* love is an action; it also makes it quite clear that *agape* love is a nonnegotiable when it comes to pleasing God. This love is so incredibly important that if we don't have it, everything else we do for God is worthless.

It doesn't matter how much doctrine we understand, how powerfully we exercise God's supernatural power, or even how much of a sacrifice we make for his kingdom; if we don't have *agape* love for others, it's all for naught.

REPENT AND DO?

Let's undo the freeze-frame and go back to Jesus' rebuke in Revelation 2. When he tells the Ephesians they've forsaken their first love, guess what Greek word is used for love?

That's right. It's *agape*. The verse says literally, "You have forsaken your first *agape*."

The problem was not that they'd lost some level of emotional zeal for God; they still had that in spades. But along the way they'd somehow stopped responding with the kind of *agape* love that put the needs and interests of others above their own; the love that had earlier enabled them to be truly forbearing with one another; the love that once had cared for and reached out to even the most ardent enemies of Christ.

Without this *agape* love, all their great deeds, doctrinal purity, hang-tough determination, and zeal to remove sin from the camp had no eternal value. They were no better than a clanging cymbal in the ears of God.

NOTICE WHAT JESUS told them to do.

He didn't tell them to come back to a certain feeling, to make him once again the strongest passion of their life.

Instead, he commanded a set of actions, actions consistent with the *agape* love they'd so freely shown in the early days. "Remember the height from which you have fallen! Repent and *do* the things you did at first."[19]

I NOW REALIZE that my early years of endlessly seeking to restore and maintain a constantly higher level of spiritual intensity and zeal for God were, frankly, misguided.

Genuine spirituality isn't found in my emotions. Neither mushy sentimentality nor rabid zeal impresses God. What he wants is simple obedience lived out in the framework of *agape* love.

Jesus put it this way:

> If you love me, you will obey what I command.... If any-one loves me, he will obey my teaching. My Father will love him, and we will come to him and make our home with him. He who does not love me will not obey my teaching. These words you hear are not my own; they belong to the Father who sent me.[20]

If our obedience comes with lots of fervor and zeal, so be it. If it comes with quiet conviction...that's okay too.

To the angel of the church in Ephesus write:

These are the words of him who holds the seven stars in his right hand and walks among the seven golden lampstands: I know your deeds, your hard work and your perseverance. I know that you cannot tolerate wicked men, that you have tested those who claim to be apostles but are not, and have found them false. You have persevered and have endured hardships for my name, and have not grown weary.

Yet I hold this against you: You have forsaken your first love. Remember the height from which you have fallen! Repent and do the things you did at first. If you do not repent, I will come to you and remove your lampstand from its place. But you have this in your favor: You hate the practices of the Nicolaitans, which I also hate.

He who has an ear, let him hear what the Spirit says to the churches. To him who overcomes, I will give the right to eat from the tree of life, which is in the paradise of God. (Revelation 2:1–7)

CHAPTER TWELVE

FENCES

Helping God Out?

I NOTICED SOMETHING ELSE in my early days as a Christian. There were lots of extra rules to follow if you wanted to count yourself among the highly committed or truly mature. It was almost as if there were two types of Christians—the stripped-down model and the gold package.

The stripped-down model trusted Jesus as Savior, went to church about once a week, and tried to follow basic biblical commands—the big stuff like the Ten Commandments.

The gold-package Christians also trusted Jesus as Savior. But they seemed to spend a lot more time at church, and they prided themselves on an impressive list of extra rules and regulations they carefully followed—all in an apparent attempt to show God and the rest of us the depth of their spiritual commitment.

REALLY TRYING

I also noticed something else about these gold-package Christians. They liked to talk about the inadequacies of the stripped-down model. It was one of their favorite subjects. From what I could gather, they weren't sure if these stripped-down versions were genuine Christians or not.

And as for unbelievers, gold-package Christians didn't seem to like them all that much either.

Every denomination and flavor of Christianity has its own set of gold-package Christians. The criteria will vary from group to group, but for all of them, the extra rules and regulations tend to share the same three goals:

1. Flee temptation.

2. Avoid any appearance of evil.

3. Steer clear of anything that might cause someone else to stumble spiritually.

Each of these issues is a big deal. That's why those who take their spirituality seriously have always been tempted to add a little extra to what's clearly laid out in the Bible. It's all in the name of an abundance of caution. If it helps God out, what can it hurt? Why not play it safe?

As a new Christian, I didn't want to be a slouch. So I tried to live up to the gold-package standards of the group that led me to Christ.

The rules were pretty straightforward: Don't drink, smoke, go to movies, dance, play cards, listen to music with "sinful" lyrics, date non-Christians, hang with non-Christians, dress worldly, or do anything else that might lead me or someone else astray.

There were even extra-credit disciplines for those who were really into it. At one point, not having a TV was a particular badge of honor. These spiritual giants traded *M.A.S.H., Seinfeld, Friends,* and the Super Bowl for extra Bible study and meditation.

I tried. I really tried. But I never could get the hang of it. From the beginning I had a haunting sense that something must be wrong with me or with our rules.

I noticed that my strict adherence to all these special rules did nothing to tame the anger, lust, temptations, and just plain selfishness residing within me.

I was also puzzled by the fact that those who were the best at keeping our code were so often the worst at humility and loving others. I mean, some of them were flat-out jerks—arrogant and perpetually angry at something or someone.

Most of all, I wondered why, if all these things were so important, God had forgotten to spell them out in the Bible. After all, he did remember to put some pretty esoteric stuff in there.

HELPING GOD OUT

One day I got up the nerve to ask my pastor why we had so many rules that weren't specifically found in the Bible.

His answer was long and convoluted. The bottom line: They were there for our safety. He saw these rules as an extra precaution, a sort of fence around God's fences to make sure we never got close enough to the edge to fall over a cliff called Sin.

I walked away realizing he didn't think God's fences were good enough. It was as if we were helping God out by building our own fences and posting a few extra *No Trespassing* and *Warning: Danger Zone* signs.

DO THESE KINDS of extra fences really make a difference? Do they help us avoid sin and temptation? Do they produce anything resembling godliness? Do they have any lasting value?

Not according to the apostle Paul.

In a letter to Christians in a town called Colosse, he once wrote:

> Since you died with Christ to the basic principles of this world, why, as though you still belonged to it, do you submit to its rules: "Do not handle! Do not taste! Do not touch!"? These are all destined to perish with use, because they are based on human commands and teachings. *Such regulations indeed have an appearance of wisdom,* with their self-imposed worship, their false humility and their harsh treatment of the body, *but they lack any value in restraining sensual indulgence.*[21]

Paul's description matches perfectly my own firsthand experiences with the extra rules and regulations of legalism. They do indeed have an appearance of wisdom. To many, they look like a higher degree of spiritual commitment. But in reality, they do nothing to restrain sin or develop godliness.

Paul's words are harsh but true. Gold-package Christianity lacks any value in restraining sensual indulgence. It just doesn't do what it's supposed to do.

IF THAT WERE the only problem with the extra fences of legalism, they would be a colossal waste of time but not particularly dangerous. But that's not their only downside. In the long run, our well-intentioned extra-biblical rules, regulations, and traditions also sabotage God's agenda in two important areas.

First, instead of protecting us from sin as advertised, they often actually *increase* the odds that we'll eventually scamper over one of his fences.

And second, instead of upholding God's reputation and honor, in reality they often end up scaring off the very people Jesus came to reach.

EMPTY THREATS

We've all seen it: the wild child whose clueless parents spout blustering warnings and ominous threats without ever actually following through.

To those of us on the outside looking in, the connection between the empty threats and the child's lack of fear and respect is obvious. But the hapless parents never seem to get it. They keep piling on dire warnings in the hopes that something might get through, while they remain oblivious to the fact that their child long ago figured out nothing bad ever happens.

The same thing occurs when we try to provide a little extra spiritual protection by posting warning signs in places God hasn't put them. Rather than helping God out, we end up undercutting his authority.

Here's why and how.

It's human nature to test the boundaries. I remember once, as a young kid, seeing a sign that warned of an electrified fence. Not wanting to get a shock, I was smart enough not to grab hold.

But I did throw a small piece of metal against it to see what would happen. When it sparked, I jumped back.

But what if the fence and warning had been placed there as an extra precaution to keep me from climbing over and getting close to the real electrified fence further inside?

I would have done the same thing. Only this time, when I threw the metal piece, there would have been no spark. Just to make sure, I would have probably thrown something else against it, or had my younger brother reach out and touch it. (Yeah, I know; but I'm just being honest.)

One thing is sure. Once I realized the warning was bogus, I would have crawled under or climbed over to see what was inside.

Now let's imagine that the owner of the fenced property had installed not one but five extra fences—to play it safe, to make sure no one ever got close enough to be shocked by the real danger inside.

After busting through the first fence, I'm sure I'd still stop and hesitate at the second. No way I'd reach out and grab it without first testing it with a small piece of metal or little brother.

Who knows? Maybe I'd do the same at the third fence. But I'm certain that by the time I hit the fourth and fifth, I'd no longer be stopping to check to see if the warnings were genuine. I'd already know they were bogus. I'd grab hold and climb over without giving it a thought.

And then—at the last fence, the real electrified fence—I'd get the shock of my life.

WHENEVER WE TRY to help out God with a few extra fences, the same thing happens. At first our warnings give pause. But it's not long until the people we're trying to protect throw some keys against the fence. Just to be sure.

I remember as a teenager being warned by my Sunday school teachers about the dangers of a host of so-called questionable behaviors. We called them the dirty dozen.

We were warned to avoid the after school dances because slow dancing would lead to lust on the dance floor, which inevitably led to fornication.

The same with alcohol—apparently a glass of merlot at dinner or a beer after work was the first step toward a life of alcoholism and misery.

While my teachers' intentions were good, the results weren't. Once a few of us had pushed the envelope—danced without losing our virginity, sipped a beer without turning into the town drunk—we learned our lesson: The warnings we heard at church were so much hot air.

Unfortunately we had no way of knowing that behind all those extra fences were other fences not to be messed with.

Sadly, some of my friends learned the hard way. Having scampered over all our extra fences with impunity, they leaped over God's fences as well, only to realize too late that his warnings are never idle.

RAISING THE BAR

The other problem with our extra rules and regulations can be found in the impact they have upon outsiders looking in. Gold-package Christianity doesn't draw people to God; it scares them away.

While outsiders might express great respect for the commitment and self-discipline shown by the gold-package folks, it's the same kind of respect most people have for someone who runs marathons, climbs Mount Everest, or notches any other high-dedication achievement: We're duly impressed, but not too likely to sign up ourselves. The price is too high.

The fact is, Jesus came to lower the entry bar, not to raise it. He's the ultimate "come as you are" Savior. Anything we do to unduly raise the bar sabotages the work he came to do.

Once we're in, the standards get pretty high. But as we saw earlier, meeting them is not something we're asked to do *before* following Jesus. It's not something we achieve on our own. It's the work of the Holy Spirit, who provides us with the power and motivation. We just follow his lead.

Unfortunately, lots of non-Christians—maybe most of them— think that *before* becoming a Christian they have to first prove their worth and commitment by living like a Christian.

Part of this is our own fault as believers. Just listen to the way many of us share our faith. How often do we focus first and foremost on some area of a person's life that's out of alignment with Scripture? We send a subtle message: Clean up your act, and then you can come to God.

We send a subtle message: Clean up your act; then you can come to God.

Now add to that all the extra rules and spiritual disciplines of our well-intended legalism. To those on the outside, this appears to raise the bar even further. It gives the impression that being a Christian means jumping through all our extra hoops and staying well behind all our extra fences.

In the days of the apostle Paul, the extra hoops and fences included asking Gentile men who wanted to follow Jesus to also become good Jews. It meant observing all the dietary, ceremonial, and religious laws of the Old Testament as well as the traditions of the elders and rabbis. And it included the ultimate herd-thinner, circumcision.

Today our extra hoops are more likely to include well-defined spiritual disciplines, avoiding certain forms of entertainment, supporting a particular political agenda, and adopting a set of so-called Christian cultural values that some would say are more in line with our nationalistic heritage than with anything found in the Bible.

And just like circumcision two thousand years ago, they thin the herd, scaring off the very people Jesus came to seek and to save.

AVOIDING THE EXTRAS

For years now I've been committed to keeping gold-package Christianity out of the church I pastor. We've worked hard to keep the bar as low as Jesus kept it. We make every effort to avoid presenting cultural values, traditions, and extra-biblical rules and regulations as if they're on par with Scripture.

As a result, we've been able to reach many people who, at first blush, wanted nothing to do with Christianity—or at least what they thought was Christianity.

We haven't had to dumb down our sermons or lower the bar of discipleship. That's just another form of trying to help God out. Instead we've let the Bible speak for itself while avoiding anything that smacks of extra rules or regulations.

One story illustrates the fruit this approach has borne.

One day, while I was studying in my office, a clearly agitated man barged in. He claimed he needed to be baptized. Right now!

I'd never met or seen him before. (We're a big church.) I asked him, "What's the big hurry?"

In quick, staccato phrases, he poured out his story. He was a new Christian. He'd just accepted a new job. He'd be moving away in a couple of weeks. And he wanted to be baptized before he left.

I thought, *This is cool*—a sort of pastor's Kodak moment. But I also wanted to know a little more of his story before going any further. So I asked him to tell me.

In essence, here's what he said:

"I didn't want to come to your church. I only came because my wife and I were having some problems. A friend said it might help.

"You don't know this, but I'm in the news business. I guess I'm part of what a lot of Christians call the 'liberal press.' I'm not exactly a Republican.

"I used to sit in the back and wait for you guys to start ripping on me and my colleagues. But you never did. In fact, I was kind of shocked. Instead, you just kept teaching the Bible. It made sense. I'd always thought the Bible was boring, narrow-minded and all. I didn't know it was so practical.

"A couple of months ago, I did what you always talk about. I stepped over the line. I gave him the steering wheel.

"And now I just took a new job with another company, and I'll be moving in a couple of weeks. So I guess I need to be baptized."

I told him I would be glad to do it.

And I couldn't help but wonder how different his story would have been if his initial exposure had been to the politics, traditions, and extra fences and hoops of gold-package Christianity. My guess is that he would have come in, taken one look around, and concluded, "I'm the enemy. I'd better get out of here. Fast."

GOD GOT IT RIGHT THE FIRST TIME

God doesn't make mistakes. He got the Bible right the first time. Nothing was left out. Nothing was forgotten. Our extra fences, hoops, and traditions not only aren't needed, they're harmful. And they certainly don't deliver on their promises.

Rather than producing God-pleasing spirituality, they're more likely to produce pride, arrogance, and self-sufficiency.

Rather than providing extra protection against sin, they increase the odds that one day we'll try to ignore his clear warnings through the mistaken assumption that they're no more valid than the empty threats posted on our man-made fences.

Rather than honoring God and keeping the church pure, they scare off the very people he's invited to come in.

Perhaps this verse from Proverbs puts it best:

> Every word of God is flawless; he is a shield to those who take refuge in him. Do not add to his words, or he will rebuke you and prove you a liar.[22]

CHAPTER THIRTEEN

BEST PRACTICES OVERLOAD

Comparison's Curse

LIKE MOST NEW CHRISTIANS, I wanted to please God. But I had no idea what that really meant—or what it looked like on a daily basis.

Trying to figure it out, I took most of my cues from two sources: (1) the Bible as I understood it, and (2) other Christians who seemed to have this God thing pretty well wired.

The Bible set the standard, while other Christians showed me how to pull it off in real life.

It was one thing to read in the Bible that I should pray about everything. It was another to observe a prayer warrior at work. The Bible motivated me; the prayer warrior showed me how. Together, they conspired to move me beyond mere conviction to actually conversing with God.

Now, years later, not much has changed. The Bible is still my foundational source for spiritual insight into God's character and eternal principles. Other Christians still provide me with working models to help me put into practice the principles of Scripture.

———

On the surface, this pattern appears to align perfectly with the Bible—with what we see in passages like these, for example:

> All Scripture is God-breathed and is useful for teaching, rebuking, correcting and training in righteousness, so that the man of God may be thoroughly equipped for every good work.[23]

> As iron sharpens iron, so one man sharpens another.[24]

> And let us consider how we may spur one another on toward love and good deeds. Let us not give up meeting together, as some are in the habit of doing, but let us encourage one another—and all the more as you see the Day approaching.[25]

But a potential danger lies hidden within this pattern of looking to the Bible and then to others to see how to live it out. The danger shows up when a well-intentioned desire to incorporate all the best traits of all the best Christians goes too far. And when it does, we can end up in the grips of what I call Best Practices Overload.

It's more common than you might think.

To understand what I mean by Best Practices Overload and its dangers and seductive nature, we need to take a short stroll down Madison Avenue and Wall Street where the concept of best practices is well known and widely pursued.

BEST PRACTICES

The term comes from the world of commerce where businesses track and follow the most successful ideas of their closest competitors—learning from their "best practices."

But it doesn't stop there. Innovative and aggressive companies don't just emulate the best practices of their own industry; they search far and wide for anyone anywhere who has a great idea or better way of doing something that might solve a problem or give them an edge over their competitors.

Hotels learned to speed up the once lengthy process of checking guests in and out by observing how car rental agencies rapidly checked out and returned cars at the airport. After all, it's far easier to steal a car than a hotel room. If the rental companies could check cars in and out so quickly, why couldn't hotels do the same with their rooms?

When General Mills needed to speed up the process of changing over a production line from one product to another, they didn't study other cereal and food companies. They already knew all their secrets. Instead, they hung out with a NASCAR pit crew for a week, looking for insights into how these guys were able to accomplish in seconds what would normally take ten to fifteen minutes.

The results were startling. After applying the lessons learned from a NASCAR pit crew to one of their production lines in California, they were able to reduce the change-over time from four and a half hours to just twelve minutes.

> This is a path you don't want to take, when it comes to improving your walk with God.

These kinds of breakthroughs are legendary in business circles. They've even fostered a micro-industry of consultants and companies who specialize in finding and analyzing the practices of the best of the best, and training other companies how to implement them.

For anyone who owns a business, the study and adoption of Best Practices is great way to ensure constant improvement and lasting success. It's a marvelous business principle.

But when it comes to improving our walk with God, it's a path you don't want to take.

Trying to follow all the best practices of all best Christians won't make you a better Christian. It might make you a nervous wreck.

Here's why.

GIFTS AND CALLING

God hasn't called us to be world-class—or even very good—at everything. Instead, he's given each of us our own unique calling together with the necessary gifting to pull it off.

Nowhere are we given the responsibility to become proficient in all the strengths and skills he's granted to others (gifts and capacities that perfectly align with *their* God-given assignment, but often have little to do with ours).

Imagine a professional golfer all worked up over his inability to consistently kick field goals. Imagine him spending hours trying to perfect the difficult skill of accurately kicking a football.

We'd question our golfer friend's sanity; write him off as a fool. Anyone gifted to be a professional golfer needs to spend the bulk of his time on the driving range and putting green, not on the gridiron trying to master the art of splitting the uprights.

Yet that's precisely what we do when we try to emulate all the spiritual disciplines and best practices of all the best Christians we've heard about or known personally.

In reality, many of those who stand out as the best example of a particular spiritual discipline, trait, or quality do so precisely because it's a significant part of what God called and gifted them to do.

We also tend to forget that many of the strengths we so admire in one person are often incompatible with the strengths we admire in another. The grace of a figure skater is useless to a sumo wrestler. The diligent research and study of my favorite theologian doesn't leave much time for the globetrotting compassion of my favorite missionary.

Spiritual heroes are great. They can call out the highest good in each of us. But too many heroes can be a problem, especially when we try to emulate each one, all at the same time.

As a new Christian, I found myself enamored with the stories of Martin Luther's prayer life, the intellect of the early church fathers, and the evangelistic prowess of Billy Graham. Though I didn't know the phrase at the time, each of them represented a spiritual "best practice."

Whenever I'd hear someone extol Martin Luther's habit of rising extra early on an over-scheduled day to get in even more prayer than usual, I'd be convicted that I wasn't praying enough, even on the slow days. Invariably I'd go home, set my alarm an hour or two early, and see if I could trade some sleep for a little extra prayer.

Then I'd listen to my favorite Bible scholar describe his study habits or those of some great theologian of the past. I'd be equally convicted. So I'd rush out, buy some heavy books, and map out a new and rigorous program for personal study.

And then I'd be exposed to the bold, passionate, and clear proclamation of the gospel from Billy Graham or some other gifted evangelist. After comparing their heart for the lost with my feeble efforts to share Christ, I'd end up feeling like a cold-hearted loser. I'd set a new goal of talking to at least one non-Christian a day about Jesus.

And then, just when I thought I was making some progress in those areas, along came Mother Teresa!

LETTING GO

At some point—I don't know exactly when—I just gave up. I decided I'd had enough of trying to live up to the best of everyone and everything.

It was a smart move.

Once I stepped back, I realized that most of my motivation to emulate all the strengths and traits I admired in others didn't come from listening to the voice of God. It came from trying to please friends and mentors who all assumed that *their* calling must be *my* calling.

I was surprised by the new sense of freedom and renewed focus I experienced once I no longer felt the need to match up to everyone else's best practices of the Christian faith. I was finally free to focus on the unique passions and gifts God had given me.

Instead of constantly feeling inadequate about the areas where I didn't match up, I started to notice and rejoice in all the areas where I did. I became a better me, rather than just a poor copy of someone else.

The fact is, God has given most of us passion and gifts for only a few things. When we follow those passions and hone those gifts, we end up doing exactly what we were made to do.

In my case, that means leading a local congregation and teaching the Bible as faithfully and accurately as I can.

And while I have much to learn from the best practices of those who excel at leadership, study, and communication, I no longer beat myself up over my failure to match up to the incredible intercessions of a prayer warrior, the eternal fruit of an evangelist, and the warm-hearted compassion of every counselor I know.

These are all wonderful things to behold. I want and need a little of each in my life. But the key phrase is *a little.*

Getting off the Best Practices Overload treadmill doesn't mean no longer learning from others or ceasing to stretch myself spiritually. There'll always be plenty of areas for growth and change. The mirror of Scripture, wise counsel, and the prompting of the Holy Spirit will see to that.

But these God-inspired areas of growth and change will for the most part align with who *we* are and what *we* have been called to do and become.

LOOKING RIDICULOUS

I'm reminded of the bizarre story of Michael Jordan, arguably the greatest basketball player of all time. Incredibly gifted at basketball, he set it all aside mid-career to seek his destiny on the baseball diamond. It made no sense. Yet there he was toiling in the minor leagues, desperately trying to learn how to hit a curve ball while the spoils and rewards of NBA championships that were his for the taking went to others.

I wonder if, in God's sight, our spiritual quest to measure up to everyone else's best traits doesn't look just as ridiculous.

As a new Christian desperately trying to match up to the best of everything spiritual, I didn't realize that the Bible spoke to the frustrations I was feeling; that it actually warned against the dangers of this trap I call Best Practices Overload:

> Now the body is not made up of one part but of many. If the foot should say, "Because I am not a hand, I do not belong to the body," it would not for that reason cease to be part of the body. And if the ear should say, "Because I am not an eye, I do not belong to the body," it would not for that reason cease to be part of the body. If the whole body were an eye, where would the sense of hearing be? If the whole body were an ear, where would the sense of

smell be? But in fact God has arranged the parts in the body, every one of them, just as he wanted them to be.[26]

A SUBTLE FORM OF REBELLION?

I've often asked myself what it is that makes us so susceptible to this thing called Best Practices Overload. Almost every Christian I know has at one time or another devalued their own gifts and calling and wished to be (or tried to be) someone else.

I've come to the conclusion that it's part of our fallen nature. At its core, it's a subtle form of rebellion against God's creative act in my life, fueled by the curse of comparison.

No matter how we slice it, there'll always be some areas of the spiritual life where we do far better than most, some where we're rather pedestrian, and some where we're destined to bring up the rear.

And just as our areas of excellence in no way excuse prideful arrogance, so too our weaker areas in no way justify a sense of spiritual inferiority, guilt, or insecurity.

If God made you an eye, being hard of hearing is no big deal. Ignore the weakness. Instead of worrying about what you can't hear, keep improving your vision.

CHAPTER FOURTEEN

GIFT PROJECTION

Chocolate-Covered Arrogance

ACCORDING TO THE APOSTLE PAUL, once we become a Christ-follower, God works in us both to *will* and to *act* according to his good purpose; he gives us both the desire and the power to carry out whatever our God-given assignment may be.[27]

That means we can expect our gifts and calling to be accompanied by a heightened awareness of the specific needs we're called to meet plus a strong internal motivation to meet those needs.

As a result, most of us have a God-given bias toward the role we're called to play. If we're called and gifted for leadership, we naturally see what needs to be accomplished—and have a strong desire to step in and get it done. If we have gifts of mercy, we probably seem to ooze empathy. If we have serving gifts, we'll tend to gravitate toward people and situations in need.

All this is well and good.

But sometimes this God-given bias goes too far. When it does, it can quickly turn into a form of spiritual arrogance that looks down on anyone who fails to share our passions and calling. It's the flip-side of Best Practices Overload.

CHOCOLATE-COVERED ARROGANCE

The most telling sign that we've crossed the line from a healthy bias to unhealthy arrogance is the presence of something called Gift Projection.

Gift Projection takes place whenever we begin to project our own unique gifts and calling upon everyone else, as if our assignment should be their assignment, and our strengths their strengths. At its core, it's an arrogant assumption that my calling is the highest calling, and my gifts are the best gifts.

I call it a chocolate-covered arrogance because on the surface it often looks like nothing more than a sincere desire and passion to carry out God's agenda. In fact, gift projectors never see it as arrogance. They think they're humbly helping God out by fervently recruiting others to a vital task.

But it's arrogance nonetheless. And God's not too hip on arrogance, even if it's chocolate coated.

MORE DRIVE-BY GUILTINGS

I once had some friends who were deeply involved in compassion ministries. They were committed to living a so-called "simple lifestyle" of low consumption, so their resources could be used to help those in far greater need.

They loved to tell stories of personal sacrifice and seemed to favor the Old Testament prophets, especially those who spoke most sternly about God's concern for justice and mercy.

Every time I was with them I'd go home feeling like a loser for not selling my car, giving the money to the poor, and taking the bus.

Another friend was a gifted evangelist. He constantly tried to motivate me and my other friends to share our faith as often and successfully as he did.

He always had amazing stories of leading complete strangers to Christ. On an airplane, in a restaurant, in a taxi, or waiting in line at the grocery store—it didn't matter where. Somehow he knew how to turn every conversation into a referendum on Jesus.

He was absolutely certain that most non-Christians were just waiting for someone to invite them to follow Christ. He was convinced that if the rest of us cared, prayed, and spoke out as boldly as he did, we too would see throngs coming to Christ

He also saw the rest of us as spiritual lightweights, unable or unwilling to join him in the only thing that had any eternal significance—evangelism.

I never quite knew how to respond.

On the one hand, I felt terribly guilty for not being concerned enough to talk to every waiter or waitress about Jesus, not to mention my failure to lead anyone to Christ between the main course and dessert.

On the other hand, I knew intuitively I could never do what he did. He easily connected and entered into deep conversations with total strangers. I had a hard time getting a waitress to bring me a second cup of coffee.

But over time I began to notice something. My evangelist friend was great at leading strangers to Christ, but he wasn't too keen about helping out with our service projects or showing up at our workdays. And anything he tried to organize or administrate quickly disintegrated into chaos.

As for his new converts, most were left to figure out the rest of their spiritual journey on their own. He thought signing them up was far more important than growing them up. When challenged about his lack of follow-up and discipleship, he'd blow it off, claiming it was God's job, not his.

Frankly, I noticed the same sort of thing with my compassion friends. They were always quick to step forward, help out, or raise money as long as the need was either desperate or far away. But they never seemed too interested in the more mundane needs closer to home. Helping out in a Sunday school class, showing up for a church workday, or giving money to keep the lights on and the staff paid were things that never seemed to make it onto their radar screen.

A TWO-WAY STREET

No one likes to be on the receiving end of a gift projector's drive-by guilting. It's disconcerting and devaluing.

I'm sure my growing awareness of others' inadequacies was due in part to my own defense mechanisms. If I could find enough faults, I could justify tuning out such people and writing them off without feeling too guilty.

But Gift Projection is a two-way street. It flows both ways. We not only let others arrogantly dump their stuff on us; we can just as arrogantly dump our stuff on them.

As I developed my own fledgling gifts of teaching and leadership, I found I could throw down some pretty good drive-by guiltings and gift projections of my own.

> I found I could throw down some pretty good drive-by guiltings and gift projections of my own.

I could nail my evangelist friend and the mercy types by playing up my long hours of study and my growing knowledge of the Bible.

If they really loved God as much as they claimed, why weren't they spending as many hours as I was studying and memorizing large chunks of Scripture? How could they claim to be serious about truth if they didn't grapple with the great theological questions of the day? Wouldn't someone who really loved God have an insatiable appetite for his word?

Yes, he should have that hunger, if he's been called to teach. But maybe not if he's been called to evangelize or work for justice and reconciliation.

Unfortunately, my gift projecting wasn't just a way to ward off the gift projections of my friends. No, the sad truth is, the more I hung around other Bible teachers and people who, like me, were preparing for professional ministry, the more I began to really believe that my assignment and gifts were the most important and valuable.

I'd learned enough to teach about the diversity of all the gifts in the body of Christ. But I hadn't matured enough to really believe it.

JUST SAY NO

To experience genuine God-pleasing spirituality, it's important to say no to any and all forms of Gift Projection.

To begin with, we can't project our stuff on others. Whenever we start to see everything and everyone through the lens of our own passions and gifts, we must learn to bite our lip and humble our heart.

That's because arrogance, even the chocolate-covered kind of Gift Projection, is a big deal. A very big deal.

God hates it.

I'M AMAZED how lightly the sin of arrogance and pride—which simply means looking down on others—is taken in so many of our Christian circles.

To struggle with pride is almost a badge of honor. Those who admit to it usually do so because they perceive themselves as having a deeper commitment, greater courage, more self-discipline, or more knowledge than the rest of us; but they claim they don't want to glory in it.

In other words, they really do think they're better.

I remember hearing a pastor speaking on humility who casually admitted his struggle with pride. While this was no news flash to anyone who knew him, it didn't seem to faze him. He might as well have said, "I struggle with driving too fast on the interstate." A flaw, but not a very big one.

But pride *is* a big deal. It's an abomination to God. In fact, when God lists the things he hates, he puts the haughty eyes of a prideful look right at the top of his list.[28]

If we want God-pleasing spirituality, we'll find our passion and gifts and go hard after them. But we'll stop short of projecting our gifts and calling on those God has assigned to a different task.

Yet, it's not enough to just avoid projecting our stuff on others. We also must learn to say no to all those who want to dump their stuff on us. God's calling comes from God, not from everyone who claims to love us and have a wonderful plan for our life.

This is especially true if your gifts and calling are neither up-front nor high-profile (which, by the way, includes the vast majority of Christians).

> So many seem to think God's kingdom would be a lot better off if only we shared their passion and calling.

The small minority of spiritual leaders who do have up-front and high-profile gifts are often the worst offenders when it comes to Gift Projection. Not because they're more arrogant than the rest of us, but because they have a greater platform from which to launch their drive-by guiltings.

Who hasn't been nailed by a missionary speaker, a powerful evangelist, or a gifted Bible teacher?

So many of them seem to think God's kingdom would be a lot better off if only we shared their passion and calling, not to mention our joining them in the priorities and spiritual disciplines they practice as a part of their calling.

I knew one pastor who chastised his congregation for being biblically illiterate. He informed them that every mature Christian should know at least the theme and basic outline of all sixty-six books in the Bible.

While that might have been particularly important for him in his role as a pastor and Bible teacher, I've still not been able to figure out how it's all that important to a Christian plumber.

Unfortunately, those with gifts of helps, mercy, administration, and other non-platform gifts never get to stand up and make the speaker types feel guilty. The result is a one-sided battle in which those with up-front gifts blast away, while everyone else ducks for cover.

THE ONE TO PLEASE

Any way you slice it, Gift Projection is a loser all around. Avoid it at all costs. It's not only ugly, it's dangerous.

To those of us who project our gifts and calling on others, it places us at odds with a God who hates haughty eyes and arrogant hearts.

To the body of Christ, it's devastating.

On the one hand it fuels and feeds the frustration of those who fall prey to Best Practices Overload by sidetracking new and insecure Christians who respond by trying to become something they were never called to be.

On the other hand, it fosters and cultivates factions in the body of Christ because Christians who share the same general gifting and calling tend to gather together to do their thing, while casting disparaging and condescending remarks toward everyone who fails to share their gifts or calling.

For all of us who have ever been on the receiving end of a gift projector's well-placed drive-by guilting, there's no reason to feel guilty or inadequate for being who God made us to be, or for doing exactly what he called us to do.

God-pleasing spirituality is found in pleasing *him*—not everyone else.

CHAPTER FIFTEEN

SEEKING BALANCE

Does God Give a Rip?

SOMEWHERE ALONG THE LINE, I picked up the goofy idea that a good Christian could and should live a perfectly balanced life.

Day to day, this meant balancing the competing tensions between work and play, family and career, spouse and kids, diet and exercise, and anything else that resided in natural tension.

In the spiritual realm, it meant finding adequate time for study, prayer, service, solitude, hanging with non-Christians, mentoring younger Christians, evangelism, discipling, cultural activism, and biblical reflection.

But it never worked very well or for very long. Like a tightrope walker forced to stay up too long, I would eventually tumble off to one side or the other.

I'd get up and try again. But I never did get the hang of it. I did manage, however, to get a nervous twitch.

WHO NEEDS IT?

Then one day, as I was bemoaning my inability to maintain the balance I so desperately sought, a well-versed friend shocked me. He claimed that the Bible nowhere calls for us to have a balanced life.

At first I thought he'd lost it. He might as well have questioned the Trinity. I mean, come on, everyone knows balance is important, especially for Christians. It's a popular topic at retreats, conferences, and Bible studies. One of the largest Christian booksellers has over 500 books with balance in the title. Amazon has nearly 8,000.

Obviously balance is important. Big-time.

But my friend pressed on. He argued that my concept of a balanced life was more a reflection of American values than anything else, and that most of the people we typically call heroes of the faith were anything but balanced.

I went home and checked. He was right.

Most of those heroes, if not all, had a single focus and lived a life that, if it were being lived out today, would be viewed as wildly out of balance—in many cases weird.

Noah, Joseph, Moses, David, Jeremiah, Daniel, Paul, Peter, Stephen, and most of the rest were all a little strange. None were what I'd call well-balanced by today's standards.

Obedient to God's call? Yes.

Balanced? I don't think so.

Noah built a nice boat. But he also had some significant family dysfunction, not to mention an issue with alcohol.

Moses was at the top of the charts as a leader, but way out of balance when it came to handling his workload. If his father-in-law hadn't stepped in, he would have worked himself to death.

David was clearly in touch with his inner self, but not as in touch with his sons—or wives. He was awfully good at carving out time for God every morning, but not so good at carving out time for them.

As for balancing work and play, if David had been on the battlefield where he belonged, the whole mess with Bathsheba would have never taken place.

Most of us would tell Jeremiah to chill out and take some Paxil. Peter would be counseled to shut up and listen more. If Paul had a life coach, he would tell the apostle to slow down and work on being less confrontational and more diplomatic.

JUST DON'T FALL OVER

My friend wasn't suggesting that we ignore areas of our life that are so out of balance they could end up causing harm either to us or to others.

The fact is, if I'm so into my work that my family begins to disconnect or disintegrate, I'm not just out of balance; I'm dangerously out of whack. And that calls for a major shift in priorities, or maybe even a change in careers.

If family and friends have become such a high priority that I have no time or concern for those outside my inner circle, something has to change. I'm not just out of balance; I'm disobeying God's command to be salt and light to my world. With zero contact, I'll have zero impact.

Such potentially fatal flaws in our character, our lifestyle, or our walk with God have to be dealt with, or they'll eventually extract a high price for our failure to deal with them.

But that's a far cry from a frantic and futile search for equilibrium in every area of life.

When we're juggling competing priorities, our ultimate goal is not to be perfectly balanced. The goal is to fulfill God's calling without falling over.

The activist Christian who volunteers at the local soup kitchen or pregnancy crisis center probably doesn't have enough time left over for a balanced regimen of aerobic exercise, serious Bible study, reflection, and journaling.

That's okay.

The Christian salesperson whose job demands lots of travel might get in plenty of spiritual reading, reflection, and journaling while stuck in an airplane, airport, or hotel room. But he'll probably fall short when it comes to fitting in time for a service project or a weekly small group Bible study.

Is our road warrior friend "out of balance"? Yes.

But does it matter? Not really.

The search for a well-balanced life tends to overlook the fact that we each have a unique calling and role to play. Playing our role well sometimes demands being out of balance somewhere else.

The quest for the bland sameness of uniformly balanced lives doesn't square with Scripture. Taken to its logical extreme, it leads to an absurd world where the eyeballs in the body of Christ try to balance their sight with better speech. It's true that eyes stink at talking. But as we discussed earlier, that's no big deal as long as they work on maintaining clear vision. The mouth will handle the speaking chores just fine.

THREE IMPORTANT QUESTIONS

I've learned to ask three important questions when it comes to juggling life's competing demands in the spiritual, physical, and workplace realms.

THE FIRST: What season is this?

Life is not static. It goes through seasons, some predictable and some catching us by surprise. Each has its own responsibilities and assignments.

During harvest the farmer had better reap. Family, friends, rest, and spiritual reflection might all be important, but if the crops aren't brought in on time, they'll rot in the field. Harvest isn't a time for balanced living. It's a time for something that looks a lot like workaholism.

The mother of two or three preschoolers has a vastly different God-given assignment while the kids are young than she'll have when her nest is empty. Trying to balance good care of the kids with consistent Bible reading, prayer, physical exercise, proper diet, time for friends, and sizzling intimacy with her husband is a recipe for fatigue and failure.

> Each season of life has its own responsibilities and assignments.

It's not going to happen.

For this mom, balance is probably out of reach. Survival is the order of the day.

THE SECOND QUESTION I like to ask: *What does God want me to do today?*

Each day has its own calling, a series of specific tasks carried out in the framework of a larger calling.

Not long after I took my friend's advice and walked away from the tyranny of seeking a fully balanced life, I began work on a graduate degree. I noticed that during the pressure-packed week of final exams, my well-balanced friends would still try to jam in all the priorities of their well-balanced life.

Those who couldn't pull it off felt guilty for neglecting all the important things on their list.

As for me, I figured my God-given assignment during finals was to do well on a series of tough exams. I intentionally let everything else go while I studied and prepped.

For five to ten days my devotional life stunk. I skipped meetings with my accountability group. Family got the short end of the stick.

I did well on the exams.

And when they were over, I found that God hadn't disowned me, the accountability group was still meeting, and my family hadn't fallen apart.

To do one thing well always means not doing so well on something else. That's why the best question to start each day with is not "What's out of balance?" It's "What does God want me to do today?"

THE THIRD QUESTION I like to ask when prioritizing life's competing demands is simply this: *Is anything so out of balance that it's beginning to harm my health, relationships, or walk with God?* That's not an easy one to answer.

The balance police will see almost any area of neglect as being critically out of alignment. To them, everything is a potential fatal flaw.

On the other hand, I'm not too likely to catch the early warning signs that something has become lopsided enough to hurt those I love or hinder my walk with God. Others may see it coming. I usually won't until after the fact.

In the end, this is a question best answered by an honest look in the mirror coupled with feedback from those who know us best.

I have a friend who married what I'll charitably call a high-maintenance wife. For him, carefully balancing work and family time is essential. It's much more important than if he'd married a more independent and secure spouse. Without it, his marriage wouldn't last.

I have another friend who's so influenced by his environment that for the sake of his walk with God, he changed careers in midlife. For him, a rigid and well-balanced schedule of work, Bible study, and family time is absolutely essential. Without it, he can't seem to stay on track.

FINDING THE SWEET SPOT

We all have different strengths and weaknesses. One man's Achilles' heel may be another man's hardened shell.

Appropriate balance can't be defined by a schedule or a checklist. It's defined by that sweet spot where we're pursuing whatever helps us play out our role better, avoiding whatever sidetracks us or causes us to fail, and ignoring most of the rest.

That's why we all have to figure out our own standard of balance. There's no rule of thumb that works for everyone. Benign neglect for you can be a fatal flaw for me.

Standing before God, we won't be asked how balanced our life was. We'll be asked how faithfully we fulfilled our calling.

In some cases, that may require a season or even a lifetime lived woefully "out of balance."

CHAPTER SIXTEEN

WHY RESULTS DON'T MATTER

Inner Peace, Success, and Failure

GREAT RELATIONSHIPS don't just happen. They take hard work and significant mid-course corrections to stay healthy over the long haul.

A relationship with God is no different.

While God never needs to grow, never makes a mistake, never misunderstands, and never chooses the selfish route, *we* do. And whenever we get off course, it usually takes some significant changes on our part to get the relationship back on track.

The problem is that we don't always know when things first start to go astray. If we blow it big-time, it's usually pretty clear. But a subtle shift into self-sufficiency, arrogance, or self-centeredness can be a lot harder to recognize.

We're all pretty good at self-deception. And it's not as if God sends us a progress report every couple of weeks.

IN OUR ATTEMPTS to figure out how we're doing spiritually, many of us look primarily to two areas to determine if we're on the right or wrong path.

We look *inside* for inner peace and a clear conscience, assuming that the absence of guilt and conviction means that everything is okay.

We look *outside* at the results of our decisions, assuming that the right ones will be blessed and successful while the wrong ones won't work out so well.

But this kind of thinking, though incredibly common, is a big mistake. Neither our conscience nor the results of our decisions are accurate measures of our spirituality or our relationship with God. Both can be incredibly deceiving.

THE PROBLEM WITH A CLEAR CONSCIENCE

We've all heard someone defend an obviously ungodly decision by saying, "I've got peace about it," as if that alone puts an end to any debate.

But inner peace and a clear conscience can't always be trusted. Prisons are full of people who followed their conscience all the way to a cold cell.

> Inner peace and a clear conscience can't always be trusted.

Unfortunately, the role of our conscience is misunderstood by many people. It's not a God-given warning system preset to go off every time we violate one of God's standards.

It's more like a thermostat we can adjust to a higher or lower temperature. Once set to the standards we believe in, it clicks in—but only when we begin to violate our own standards, not God's.

That's why we can all identify actions and behaviors that we once thought to be wrong but now believe to be right, or that we once considered perfectly fine but now view as terribly wrong.

In each case, our conscience was recalibrated and reset to a new standard. Ideally, these changes are the result of aligning our values with the values of Scripture. But it's no secret that our conscience can just as easily be reset to align with our actions, providing cover for things we once knew to be wrong but now find ourselves caught up in.

THE PROBLEM WITH RESULTS

Results can be equally deceiving. Whether I'm succeeding or failing has little or nothing to do with whether I'm on the right path.

Yet most of us tend to judge our relationship with God by how things are going. When everything goes well, we assume we're on pretty good terms. If we're on a roll, it's because he's really pleased. When the roof caves in, we wonder what we did to tick him off.

But success and failure reveal nothing about our spirituality. Even being used mightily by God is not a sure sign we're on good terms.

Think of Job's run of bad luck or Samson's run of good luck. Based on the visible short-term results, we'd never guess that Job was the apple of God's eye or that Samson was displeasing God with his pursuit of forbidden women, while still winning great battles for God.

I know, Samson's sins eventually caught up with him. But even then, God granted him power for one last devastating defeat over his enemies.

And yes, Job got back double what he lost. But no one I know would sign up for his investment strategy. When you're one of the richest guys in the world, there's not much to gain by going double or nothing (or more accurately, nothing then double).

The results I'm experiencing—whether good, bad, or ugly—prove nothing. God's plan and handiwork have always been hard to see in the moment. They're best viewed and evaluated through life's rearview mirror, often long after we've passed through a particularly treacherous valley or enjoyed the pleasures of fleeting success.

The only sure and reliable sign that I'm on good terms with God is my obedience to his commands and laws. This alone proves that I know him and love him.

According to the apostle John, "We know that we have come to know him if we obey his commands. The man who says, 'I know him,' but does not do what he commands is a liar, and the truth is not in him."[29]

As Jesus himself said, "If you love me, you will obey what I command."[30]

SEDUCED BY SUCCESS

Admittedly, in some cases success can be a legitimate sign of God's favor.

For instance, the book of Proverbs contains many passages that make a strong connection between living a righteous life and enjoying God's blessing and overall life success.

But these are proverbs, not promises. They're statements about how life generally works, not promises about what always happens.

That's why the book is called Proverbs, not Promises.

Consider Stalin's long and successful political career. Or the lengthy reign of Fidel Castro. Even Hitler had great success for many years. Fortune 500 companies aren't generally known to be run by pious Christians. The great generals of antiquity were hardly saints. Sometimes the good die young. Sometimes the bad guys win.

Success's great miscalculation is the assumption that it *always* springs from God's favor—and the greater the success, the greater his favor.

The truth is, success springs from many sources. God's favor may or may not be one of them.

Most Christians know this—on an intellectual or theological level. But the connection between success and God's blessings is so deeply ingrained that when real life happens, we quickly forget.

That's why the disciples, who knew well the story of Job, were so shocked when Jesus spoke of a rich man having a hard time entering the kingdom of God. They couldn't get past the natural assumption that great riches were the product of God's great favor.

But perhaps the classic tale of a good and godly man misinterpreting his success can be found in the biblical account of a king named Uzziah. You'll want to read the whole story.[31] But for now, here's the short version.

Uzziah became king at age sixteen. He got off to a great start. Spiritually, he sought the Lord and did the right thing. Politically and militarily, he showed great wisdom and experienced phenomenal success.

As the boundaries of his kingdom expanded, his fame spread. Decades of peace, a powerful and well-equipped army, and his enormous wealth put him in a Solomon-like category.

But with his great success came a creeping sense of being so specially favored by God that the rules for other kings didn't apply to him. I don't mean the rules about moral purity, honesty, and integrity; he apparently kept those well. No, the rules that didn't make sense to Uzziah had to do with religious ceremonies and spiritual protocol.

He took it upon himself to fulfill a previously forbidden role, the role of a king/priest—a role God had reserved exclusively for the coming Messiah.

I can imagine what Uzziah was thinking: I'm God's man. Just look at how he's blessed me. Why do I need to go through these priests? Why can't I offer my own sacrifice of incense? I'm far closer to God than they are. Just look at how he's blessed me.

So Uzziah picked up a censer and went into the temple, planning to honor God by personally burning a sacrifice of incense to his Lord.

But as soon as he entered the temple and picked up the censer, the high priest and eighty other courageous priests stepped forward to stop him.

Uzziah burned with rage. How could they think for a minute that his sacrifice would not be honored by the Lord? Just look at how God had blessed him.

But as he raged against the priests, leprosy broke out on Uzziah's forehead.

At that point, he suddenly decided it was time to leave the sanctuary. But it was too late.

Here's the tragic description of what followed:

> King Uzziah had leprosy until the day he died. He lived in a separate house—leprous, and excluded from the temple of the LORD. Jotham his son had charge of the palace and governed the people of the land… Uzziah rested with his fathers and was buried near them in a field for burial that belonged to the kings, for people said, "He had leprosy."[32]

Here was a king whose epitaph should have read, "Here lies Uzziah, the great king who brought us decades of peace and prosperity."

Instead it read, "Here lies Uzziah. He had leprosy."

It could just as well have said, "Here lies Uzziah. He was seduced by success."

FOOLED BY FAILURE

But success isn't the only thing that can cause us to misunderstand our relationship with God and do some really stupid things. So can failure.

When things fall apart, most of us assume there has to be a reason. We start looking for the lesson to be learned or the sin to be removed.

If we can't find anything deserving of God's discipline, we figure that some day soon we'll see how this bad thing was really a good thing, a necessary part of our spiritual growth or future success.

That's why we find it so confusing when we face a major defeat or failure without any seeming connection to sin, or any possible good that we can imagine coming out of it. We begin to question God's goodness and faithfulness. Our deeply ingrained assumption that failure must mean something is spiritually wrong makes it nearly impossible to accept the idea that we can fail when everything is spiritually okay.

But isn't that the lesson of the book of Job?

Job was God's pride and joy. According to a bizarre and unexplained scene in the first chapter, God asks Satan if he's noticed his main man, Job, who God then goes on to describe as being blameless and upright.

So what was Job's reward for this attention? The well-known trials of Job—the epitome of unexplained suffering.

INTERESTINGLY, Job's friends were a lot like us. They didn't think his suffering was so hard to understand. They assumed it was a clear sign that God was upset with Job about something.

The bulk of the book centers on their musings and suggestions as to why Job was in such a mess, and Job's strident defense of his character and spirituality.

Toward the end of the book, God shows up again. He shuts up Job's friends with a series of tough questions they can't answer. He then tells them to have Job pray for them. Then he leaves, never having answered the "why" question.

But he did make one thing clear: Job's tragic circumstances had nothing to do with God's displeasure. Quite the contrary. In God's eyes, there was no one like or equal to Job in all the earth.

The fact is, in the midst of a trial or failure (unless we can see some direct connection to specific sinful choices), we can't know what it means.

In Job's case, the stuff happening to him was more about us than about Job. He learned a few things, lived a lot longer, then died. I'm not sure it did much more for him than create some difficult and confusing memories.

But since then, countless millions have found comfort and understanding in the book that bears his name. Who's to say Job ever had a clue his story would help so many?

A VALLEY DOESN'T MEAN A WRONG TURN

Judging God or my spiritual journey by results also tends to ignore the fact that the middle of a story is never the end of the story.

At one point, Moses would have been judged a loser with a grandiose vision that far exceeded God's actual calling. Pharaoh wouldn't listen. Things got worse for the people Moses came to deliver. Plagues designed to show God's power were easily duplicated by the Egyptian magician. Moses' own people wanted him voted out of office.

Yet despite what the results seemed to imply, he was right where God wanted him to be, doing exactly what God wanted him to do. Moses was in a valley. But it didn't mean a wrong turn.

The same goes for David and his fugitive years. Life on the lam, running from an insanely jealous king, isn't what we'd expect of God's anointed and rightful ruler. It hardly looks like the sweet spot of God's will. But it was. David, too, was in a valley. But it didn't mean a wrong turn.

The last week of Jesus' life became a disaster. Adulation and acceptance as the Messiah suddenly turned into rejection, false accusations, betrayal, and a limp, lifeless body on a cross. He was in a valley. But it didn't mean a wrong turn.

> Whenever we let our failures become the determiner of God's character, we'll inevitably come to some wrong conclusions.

Sunday was coming.

We're no different. Whenever we let our failures, both short-term and long-term, become the determiner of God's character or the condition of our spiritual walk, we'll inevitably come to some wrong conclusions. Then we'll just as certainly make some wrong decisions—the most common of which will be running from the valley, even when it's right where God wants us to be.

SUCCESS, FAILURE, and inner peace don't tell me much when it comes to measuring my spirituality or my relationship with God.

But as we've seen over and over, doing the right thing and obeying his commands does. It remains the best way to know how I'm doing, and how to stay in the center of God's will.

Faith and obedience always matter.

Results don't.

CHAPTER SEVENTEEN

PREPARING THE HORSE

Lessons from the Unseen Realm

WHEN I BECAME the pastor of North Coast Church I was 28 years old. For a month or two everything was great.

Then the wheels came off.

People who had enthusiastically supported me when I candidated became fierce critics after I arrived. Changes I'd been asked to make, once made, were firmly resisted and even sabotaged.

It was a small church, just a couple of years old. We met in a high school cafeteria. After an initial growth spurt, I was pleased to see us averaging 150 in weekend attendance (that's counting adults, children, and anyone who accidentally drove through the parking lot).

Three years later, we were at 151, an annual growth rate of one-third of a person per year—hardly what the board had in mind when they asked me to become their pastor.

We did get some new people. But for every new person who came, someone else left, usually upset and mad about something. I got a lot of phone calls that began, "Pastor, you know I love you, but…" Which is Christianese for "You aren't going to like what I say next."

I still think of that time as the Dark Years. Though my health, my marriage, and the important things of life were all going well, I was consumed by the failure I was experiencing in my chosen profession. I was sure the elders were going to fire me any day. And I knew the track record and resume I was building would hardly make me a desirable candidate for another church in another town.

SLEEPLESS IN SAN DIEGO

During those early years it was rare for me to sleep through the night. Looking back, I realize I was depressed and frightened, though too insecure to admit it.

A major factor was that I'd never experienced significant failure before. In my previous ministry settings I'd been the golden boy, precocious and successful beyond my years. But like many who experience a good deal of success early on, I thought *I* was the one who created it. I figured the reason things went well was that, compared to the next guy, I was more committed, I was smarter, or I just worked harder.

Now here I was three years into my chosen career without any hint of the success I'd known earlier. Apparently I wasn't as talented, godly, or committed as I'd thought.

DEPRESSION'S ARROGANCE

Then one day I had a huge spiritual epiphany. I don't remember when or how it came, but it dawned on me so suddenly and clearly that I felt stupid for not having seen it before.

I realized that the thought patterns causing me to be so depressed over our church's lack of growth and ministry success were exactly the same thought patterns that would have made me big-headed and arrogant if things had gone well.

I was taking too much blame for my lack of success in much the same way I'd taken too much credit for my previous victories. My discouragement was rooted in the same value system and paradigm as pride; it just had different data to work with.

AS WE SAW in the previous chapter, results don't always matter in the spiritual realm. They can't be trusted as an accurate measure of God's approval or disapproval.

But does that also mean they can't tell me anything about how well I'm doing my job? And if results don't matter, what does God hold me responsible for? Is it enough to just go through the motions and then step back to see what happens? Or am I in some way responsible to work hard to set the table for victory and success?

PREPARING THE HORSE

Around the same time I came across two verses in the book of Proverbs that helped put these questions into perspective. They profoundly altered the way I approach and view my personal responsibilities and the way I evaluate and assess my victories and defeats.

As I've mined their depths, they've become a sort of North Star that I use to keep me on track as I pursue my daily assignment from God. Whether I'm working on a small project, a large initiative, or my life mission, they've helped me to keep focused, and not to run away every time the weeds get deep or to puff up with self-important pride whenever success shows up.

Here they are:

> There is no wisdom, no insight, no plan that can succeed
> against the LORD. The horse is made ready for the day of
> battle, but victory rests with the LORD.[33]

A man named Asaph learned a lesson similar to what I learned about preparing the horse. His journey unfolds in Psalm 73.

As he looked around, he noticed that life was hardly fair. While he and his God-fearing companions faced tough times and apparent defeats, the wicked seemed to be without worry or struggle. He was jealous of their prosperity, health, and carefree lifestyle.

What he saw in his surrounding circumstances caused him to nearly chuck it all: "Surely in vain have I kept my heart pure; in vain have I washed my hands in innocence" (verse 13).

Have you ever felt that way? I sure have. Most anyone has, if they've experienced such undeserved struggles as facing significant injustice or a life-threatening illness.

In the dark shadows of those valleys, we all have a natural tendency to judge God and our spiritual journey based on the latest returns.

But God showed Asaph something that completely changed his perspective. God showed him what ultimately awaited the wicked; he showed Asaph "their final destiny" (verse 17). Here was the final chapter, the last page that was yet to come—not the mid-story scene that Asaph was currently living through.

God showed him their end.

Suddenly Asaph realized that the wicked stood on slippery ground. It was only a matter of time until their footing gave way—if not in this life, then certainly in the next.

No longer ready to toss it all, no longer wondering if he'd wasted his time on the wrong path; Asaph begins to praise God for his faithfulness and to marvel at the folly of his earlier short-term judgments. The end result was one of the great psalms in the Bible.

The passage reminded me that final outcomes are in the hands of the Lord. It's his will that prevails. There's no wisdom, insight, or plan that can thwart it, whether mine or my enemy's.

But it also clearly pointed out the one thing I *could* control, and by inference, the one thing I'll be held responsible for: How well was I preparing my horse for battle?

It caused me to realize that during my Dark Years I was asking the wrong question.

I asked, "How are things going?"

I should have asked, "Am I doing the right things? Am I preparing my horse for victory?" In the end, that's all I have any control over.

IN THE UNSEEN REALM

A look at two of Joshua's battles in the book that bears his name helps to explain how this works out—how our role and God's role intersect.

It also reveals the impact and power of the unseen realm upon our endeavors, an influence and power most of us fail to factor in adequately when judging our victories and defeats.

The story of these two battles can be found in Joshua chapters six through eight. Here's what we find.

Joshua had been given the responsibility to lead the children of Israel into the Promised Land. His first assignment was to wage battle against a large and well-fortified city called Jericho.

But God didn't want this to be any old victory; it must be one that could be credited only to his power and protection. So he commanded Joshua's army to march around the city for seven days; on the last day, when the priests blew their trumpets and the people shouted, God would knock down the walls.

The Lord also laid down one special rule. All the iron, gold, silver, and bronze from Jericho was to be put aside into his treasury. It all belonged to him. After Jericho, all the spoils of any future victories would belong to the soldiers. But the first fruits of their success belonged to God.

Everything went according to plan. The people marched, the priests blew their trumpets, and all the spoils were gathered and set aside for the temple treasury.

The next town to be conquered was a small and insignificant outpost called Ai. Joshua sent a much smaller army to do the honors. To everyone's shock and dismay, God's army was routed. Thirty-six men were lost in the battle.

Nothing was wrong with their battle plan at Ai. Nothing was wrong with the army that went to battle. Nothing was wrong with the thirty-six brave soldiers who died.

But something was dreadfully wrong in the unseen realm. It was something they had no way of knowing about, no way to overcome.

The battle was lost and thirty-six men died because one idiot named Achan decided God's rule about the Jericho spoils didn't apply to him. When no one was looking, he stashed away two hundred shekels of silver and a wedge of gold and hid them under his tent.

There are things in the unseen realm we'll never know or understand.

Because of Achan's sin, thirty-six families lost a son, father, or husband. Those slain men and their grieving families weren't responsible for Achan's actions; they were simply caught in the backwash of his sin. It was a battle lost in the unseen realm.

I've heard people criticize Joshua for his presumption in sending such a small portion of his army. But a bigger army would have only meant a bigger defeat. In this situation there was no wisdom, insight, or plan that could have succeeded; the Lord had deter-

mined to punish the nation for the sins of one man. It was his pre-
rogative to do so. He did so.

The lesson of their defeat is incredibly important to us today.
It's especially relevant to those of us brought up with an American
or Western emphasis on the rights and responsibilities of the individual. We're already too quick to gloss over the implications of our
interconnectedness. Add to that a mechanistic view of the world
that often downplays the unseen realm, and you have a recipe for
disillusionment and confusion when battles that should have been
won are lost.

GETTING CLARITY ABOUT CONTROL

Taking the insights of Proverbs and the lessons of the defeat at Ai,
I've learned to pay a lot less attention to outcomes.

I've found there's a certain steadiness and emotional equilibrium that comes with understanding the difference between my
role and God's. Defeats aren't as devastating. Victories aren't as
seductive.

I've also found tranquility in accepting the fact that there are
things in the unseen realm I'll never know or understand. It keeps
my brain from overheating with hyper-analysis every time things
don't go according to plan.

Not that I don't ask why and how it happened, and what we
can do differently next time. I'll always ask those questions. They're
important. But I've also come to accept that sometimes they won't
have answers.

At times, we're not much different from the soldiers who
marched out to conquer Ai. If there's an Achan in the camp, we
can figuratively (and in some cases literally) die—through no fault
of our own.

We take too much credit when the walls of Jericho cave in

and too much blame when our Ai's can't be conquered.

What God wants for us is to simply focus our energy and efforts on the one and only thing we *can* control, the one and only thing God will hold us accountable for: How well have we prepared the horse for battle?

After that, I've learned, it's God's call—not ours.

CHAPTER EIGHTEEN

TOOLS OR RULES?

Finding What Works for You

You don't have to be a Christian long before you notice how everyone seems to have a favorite recipe for promoting spiritual growth.

While the details of a particular formula may vary from one church or denomination to another, most are drawn from a relatively small universe of widely accepted spiritual disciplines.

As you'd expect, enthusiasm for a particular discipline or practice often flows out of personal experience. Something's made a profound difference in our life, so we encourage others to give it a try.

But a surprising number of people also recommend and swear by things that *ought* to work but never have really worked for them. This seems to be particularly true among authority figures—pastors, teachers, parents, and Sunday school leaders.

For instance, I've heard lots of speakers claim that prayer is an essential element in a successful marriage, that the couple who prays together stays together. Only to find out later that the person pontificating about the need for prayer hardly ever prayed with their own spouse—and had a strong marriage anyway.

The same often goes for what they say about daily Bible reading, early morning prayer, journaling, memorizing Scripture, solitude, family devotions, involvement in a small group, private acts of servanthood, and more.

So what's the truth? Are these things essential or not?

On one hand I've known lots of people who have greatly benefited by putting them into practice. On the other hand, I've known plenty of people (I bet you have too) who ignored these so-called "essential" spiritual disciplines, or applied them only sporadically, and who nonetheless seemed to have an enviable walk with God.

TOOLS OR RULES?

Unfortunately, those who champion a particular spiritual discipline or practice usually do so in a way that makes it sound like a non-negotiable. It's presented as an essential rule of the game, ignored only at great peril.

Yet the Scriptures paint a different picture. They don't present spiritual disciplines as rules. They present them as tools to help us know and follow God better.

There's no question that the standard disciplines and recipes for spiritual growth have legitimate biblical support. Most are modeled throughout.

But upon further review, few, if any, rise to the level of a biblical command. And that alone puts them in the category of a tool, not a rule.

THE DIFFERENCE between a tool and a rule is profoundly important. Rules must be obeyed, all the time, by everyone. No exceptions.

Tools are different. They're task-specific. A hammer is a wonderful device. When I need to pound a nail into a piece of wood, it's indispensable. But if I'm trying to polish glass, it's best left in the toolbox.

There's no value in using any tool for the tool's sake. If it helps accomplish the task, it's a wise choice. If it doesn't, it's a foolish choice.

The same goes for the spiritual tools we've come to call spiritual disciplines.

WHY DO WE TURN TOOLS INTO RULES?

I've long pondered why we have such a strong propensity to turn the powerful tools of spiritual discipline into the lifeless rules of religious ritual.

I've come to believe that two things in particular work against us.

THE FIRST is our natural tendency to project our personal experiences onto everyone else. As we saw earlier while exploring the dangers of Gift Projection, it's a hard habit to break.

When my wife had cancer, it seemed like everyone who had beaten it, or knew someone who had beaten it, had a magic cure they wanted her to take or follow. We were inundated with emails, articles, suggestions, products, and jars of who knows what. Everyone was certain that what worked for them would work for us.

It's no different in the spiritual realm. When something profoundly changes our life, most of us are fairly certain it would do the same for anybody, if given the chance.

THE SECOND PROBLEM is our tendency to confuse the prescriptive with the descriptive.

The Bible contains many prescriptive passages—the commands and exhortations that tell us what to do.

But it also contains many descriptive passages that simply describe what someone did.

The problem arises when we treat every passage as if it's prescriptive. This turns every narrative about a godly person or hero of the faith into a template we must follow rather than a model we can learn from. And that's a mistake.

The descriptive passages of the Bible contain treasure troves of spiritual insights and principles, but they don't necessarily insist that we do the same thing. We just assume they do.

For instance, when the Bible says that God considered King David a man after his own heart, we naturally look to see what David did, because we also want to be a person after God's own heart.

We find that he drew close to God by rising early, memorizing and meditating on Scripture, and journaling and expressing his feelings and spiritual insights through song and poetry. We see that he gave great sums of his wealth to the temple and refused to carry out his own revenge against his nemesis, King Saul.

But we also find that he started out as a shepherd. That he had multiple wives. That he faked his way out of a dangerous situation by pretending to be insane. That he lived in a time without electricity.

So which of these things are prescriptive, and which are merely descriptions of what David did?

If his worship patterns found in the Psalms are prescriptive, shouldn't tending sheep be a prerequisite to spiritual leadership?

As for his early morning meetings with God, could the lack of electricity and late-night meetings have something to do with his getting up at the crack of dawn? And isn't it likely that his artistic bent had something to do with the emotive nature of his psalms and his walk with God?

WHAT IS NEW TESTAMENT CHRISTIANITY?

Similar issues pop up when we come to the New Testament. I've heard lots of people and churches claim to be "New Testament Christians."

I'm never quite sure what they mean.

If they mean following the commands of Jesus and the New Testament letters, I'm in. If they mean trying to follow all the patterns of New Testament life found in the book of Acts or the Epistles, I'm not so sure.

Once again, who decides what to include and what to exclude? And on what basis? The choices often seem rather arbitrary.

As an example, take the story in Acts of the expansion of the early church. Here's what it tells us about life in the church after the great outpouring of God's Spirit on the day of Pentecost:

> They devoted themselves to the apostles' teaching and to the fellowship, to the breaking of bread and to prayer. Everyone was filled with awe, and many wonders and miraculous signs were done by the apostles. All the believers were together and had everything in common. Selling their possessions and goods, they gave to anyone as he had need. Every day they continued to meet together in the temple courts. They broke bread in their homes and ate together with glad and sincere hearts, praising God and enjoying the favor of all the people. And the Lord added to their number daily those who were being saved.[34]

This passage is clearly descriptive. It tells us what they did. There are no commands. Yet it's almost always taught as a prescription for how *we* ought to do church, rather than a description of how *they* did church. It's become a template to follow rather than an example to learn from.

I find it fascinating to observe who leaves out what when they teach this passage. Most everyone claims that we need to emulate the early Christians' devotion to the apostles' teachings, fellowship, the Lord's Supper, and prayer.

But my charismatic friends also include their sense of awe as well as signs and wonders.

Most of my Baptist friends don't.

Old hippies and those who live in a communal setting like to emphasize how the first Christians lived together and had everything in common.

Most suburbanites don't.

Those who are heavy into mercy ministries and a simple lifestyle favor the verses about selling all their possessions and sharing with anyone in need.

Most Christian investment counselors don't.

And everyone seems to give a free pass on the requirement to meet daily, especially in the courts of the Jerusalem temple.

These kinds of inconsistencies are inevitable when we try to turn the descriptive into the prescriptive—when we take powerful tools and try to make them universal rules.

The patterns of spiritual discipline found in the Scriptures and in the "best practices" of God's people down through the ages are incredibly informative and helpful. Following in their footsteps can often draw us closer to God.

But it's important to remember that when it comes to spiritual disciplines, we're dealing with tools, not rules. As powerful as they can be, tools have no value in themselves. Their value is in what they produce.

THE DIFFERENCE A TOOL MAKES

As I've learned to treat the standard spiritual disciplines as tools rather than rules, I've found them to be much more powerful.

Depending on what I need to accomplish or build into my life, I'll look through my spiritual toolbox and pick out just the right one for the task at hand. When applied to the right situation at the right time, it will get the job done.

For instance, years ago I decided I needed to better understand the big picture of Scripture. So I started memorizing portions of it.

To help me keep going on the days I didn't feel like it, I found a partner to join me in the task.

I began with little memory cards, memorizing hundreds of individual verses. That soon morphed into memorizing entire books of the New Testament, particularly any book I was about to teach.

The results were powerful. I began to see things I'd never seen before. I no longer talked about the larger context of a passage; I *saw* it. I became much more biblical in my thinking, more insightful in my teaching.

But eventually, my daily habit of memory work stopped bearing the same fruit. It had taught me to look at Scripture in a new way. It had taught me to think with new paradigms. But fresh insights were now few and far between. The energy expended no longer seemed worth it.

So I stopped.

My memory partner was aghast. For him, the tool had become a rule. He was sure I would soon begin a slow slide away from God, that any wisdom and spiritual insights I'd gained would atrophy away.

Looking back, I realize he'd taken the discipline of Scripture memory down a path that's all too common.

What started out as a useful tool to help him know God

became in his mind the most important tool of all (not only for him, but also for everyone else). From there it was a short step to making memorization an end in itself, the measure by which he gauged his walk with God and mine as well.

> What started out as a useful tool became an end in itself—the measure by which he gauged his walk with God.

But for me, Scripture memory was simply a tool. It had served its purpose. I now had new areas to work on. It was time to put the straight-edge of Scripture memory away and pick up another tool, one designed to help me accomplish the next task at hand.

FINDING WHAT WORKS FOR YOU

Once we cast aside the idea that the spiritual disciplines are mandatory rituals and rules, we're free to pick up and use whatever tool best fits the need of the moment.

Here are some general guidelines that have helped me develop a useful toolbox and determine what tools to use when:

TRY THEM ALL. I've found great benefit in trying as many as possible. There are few recipes for spiritual growth that I haven't tried. I've taken a shot at everything from fasting to solitude, from setting my alarm clock for early morning prayer and Bible study to performing secret acts of service. I try different disciplines because it helps me know what's out there and available.

KEEP WHAT WORKS. If these were rules, it wouldn't matter whether they worked. But since they're tools for spiritual growth, the first thing I ask is, "Is this working?"

If the answer is yes, I keep after it. If the answer is no, I set it aside for later.

In a few cases, I've tried a particular spiritual discipline or practice enough times to know that it simply doesn't have my name on it. So I've set it aside for good.

When family devotions bored my kids, we put it (and them) to bed. Better to have a few friends think I'm a terrible father for not reading the Bible to my children than to have them grow up thinking of God as terminally boring.

Be honest. I find it helpful to regularly ask, "Where do I most need to grow?"

Sometimes I can see it myself; sometimes I need to listen to those who know me best. But one or two areas always stand out above the rest. Knowing what they are helps me pick the right tool for the situation.

I've also noticed that my spiritual life goes through various seasons, ebbs and flows that sometimes come full circle. I've actually had two seasons when memorizing Scripture jumped to the forefront. Each time I sensed the inner prompting of the Holy Spirit to give it a whirl. So I did. Each time it made a big difference— for awhile. When the season passed, I put the tool back in the toolbox.

Know yourself. Our individual personality and makeup greatly impacts what works for us and what doesn't work. That's why the same tool applied to a similar situation doesn't always produce the same results.

If you thrive on routine, you probably feel most alive when things are most in order. The more regimented disciplines will likely make the greatest difference in your life. It would be no surprise if you found your greatest help in life-long patterns.

But if anything that lasts more than six weeks feels to you like a straightjacket, you'll probably rotate through the disciplines in a manner that your more scheduled friends will see as undisciplined and flighty.

No matter. They're just tools. Find the ones that work best for you and put them to work. It's okay to leave the rest in the toolbox for now—ready to serve you when the right time comes.

CHAPTER NINETEEN

THE POTENTIAL TRAP

Why Being All We Can Be Might Be a Dumb Idea

FOR YEARS the United States military poured millions of dollars into a recruiting campaign built around the simple statement, "Be all that you can be."

It proved to be an incredibly powerful marketing slogan, resonating with the conventional wisdom of our age, a wisdom that proclaims maximizing our potential as one of life's sacred responsibilities.

I find most Christians drink from the same cup.

We tend to see unfulfilled potential as a tragic shame; squandered opportunity as a sinful choice. We assume that God couldn't possibly be pleased with anyone who settles for being less than the best they can be—in any area of life.

But it's a lie.

Potential is not a sacred responsibility.

Potential is a harsh mistress—seductive, never satisfied, prone to exaggeration, nearly impossible to figure out. Those who pursue her inevitably end up in the poisoned land of self-centered priorities and me-first decisions.

But it's a quest that's often justified with pious platitudes about following God's calling and using all the gifts we've been given.

However, God's highest calling won't be found there. It's found on another path, far removed from the "me-first" orientation of the maximized potential crowd. It's found on a seldom traveled side-road filled with opportunities for sacrifice, service, and self-denial.

STRANGE INTERPRETATIONS

The siren call of fully realized potential has become so powerful that it's now commonly read into biblical passages written more than a millennium before the ideas of Maslow and the self-help gurus were even thought of.

Even the straightforward decree to "love others as we love ourselves" has been turned into a plea for more self-focus. Apparently,

Destination sickness:

Another problem with the quest to use all our gifts and fulfill all our promise, no matter what, is that it sets us up for the heartache known as Destination Sickness.

There's nothing worse than arriving where you wanted to go, only to realize you don't want to be there. We've all experienced it at some level—having left something good for what we thought was much better; only to find that the greener grass was painted concrete.

But perhaps the saddest part of the journey to bogus greener grass is that it almost always leaves behind broken relationships. Co-workers, family members, friends, and those who depend on us are devastated to discover that our deepest loyalty is not to them, but to ourselves and our potential.

the more I learn to put myself first, the greater capacity I'll have to love others.

But let's be real. We don't have any problem putting ourselves first. We come by that quite naturally.

We may struggle with poor self-esteem, the leftover baggage of a dysfunctional family or an inability to set healthy boundaries. But we definitely don't need anyone to teach us how to be more selfish and self-centered.

Adam took care of that.

THEN THERE'S the famous Parable of the Talents that Jesus taught. This passage is often used to stress the need for making the most of our God-given talents. It's become the quintessential passage on maximizing our potential.

In the parable,[35] Jesus tells of a man who goes on a long journey, entrusting his property and assets to three servants. When he comes back, one of the servants has turned five talents into ten; another has turned two into four.

But the third servant, who was given just one talent, has done nothing to increase his allotment. He simply buried it for safekeeping, waiting to dig it up when his master returned.

The two servants who doubled their funds are praised and amply rewarded. But the one who failed to make an increase finds himself in a world of trouble.

Jesus quotes their master's response:

> You wicked, lazy servant!... You should have put my money on deposit with the bankers, so that when I returned I would have received it back with interest. Take the talent from him and give it to the one who has the ten talents. For everyone who has will be given more, and he

will have an abundance. Whoever does not have, even what he has will be taken from him. And throw that worthless servant outside, into the darkness, where there will be weeping and gnashing of teeth.[36]

That got my attention as a new Christian. I didn't want to go to hell. I didn't want what little I had to be taken away and given to another. So I determined to maximize to the fullest any and every talent God had given me.

This soon became my primary grid for making major life decisions. Relationship, career, and educational commitments were all made or broken based on whether they furthered or hindered my pursuit to be all I could be for God.

At the time, it made a lot of sense. My culture already screamed that unrealized potential was a tragic waste. Now the Bible seemed to confirm it.

But I was headed down the wrong path.

The parable I based it all on didn't actually say what I'd been told it said. It didn't mean what I thought it meant.

While it might hold some general applications to how we use our gifts and talents, that's not what the Parable of the Talents is all about.

It's not a warning about unfulfilled potential. It's a warning about ignoring a God-given assignment and doing nothing to advance the cause of the master.

The difference is significant.

SOME OF THE confusion stems from a rather unfortunate linguistic twist. In the days of Jesus, a talent was a Roman monetary measurement. It had nothing to do with skills and abilities. Jesus' original hearers would have thought primarily in terms of a fiduciary responsibility to care for the master's property.

But English speakers immediately think of a talent in terms of God-given abilities, skills, and capacities. That's how we use the word. The idea of a specific assignment or monetary entrustment is way down the list.

So, not wanting to share the same fate as the unfortunate sap who buried his talent, most of us surmise that we'd better get with it and start striving harder to maximize any gifts and talents that have yet to reach their full potential.

THE PROBLEMS WITH POTENTIAL

Actually, my disillusionment with the pursuit of fully realized potential began long before I knew anything about Roman coinage or the language and context of the New Testament.

It started with a little fruit inspecting.

I noticed that my friends and colleagues who considered fulfilling their personal potential as the best way to please God were *not* becoming more Christlike. They were becoming increasingly competitive, self-centered, and dissatisfied.

I also noticed that when it came time to make major life decisions, the compass called potential always pointed to the bigger platform, the more challenging task, and the greater rewards. It seldom pointed toward sustaining a long-term relationship, a slower pace, a lesser role, or an old-fashioned concept called loyalty.

SELF-DECEPTION

Another problem with chasing potential is that it can be a tough read. It's incredibly hard to get an accurate assessment.

Despite all the talk about an epidemic of low self-esteem, the facts don't support the myth. Research continually shows that the vast majority of us have a rather inflated view of our talents, relational skills, and leadership gifts—something that obviously impacts our self-perceived sense of potential.

I saw one survey of over 150,000 college students where everyone—that's right, every single person—rated themselves as above average in their ability to get along with others. That means at least 75,000 of them were mildly to seriously delusional!

In my own profession, some surveys show that up to 80 percent of pastors rate their preaching skills as well above average. Our congregants aren't so kind; 60 percent say our messages aren't so hot—rating them as average or below.

The same thing happens nearly anywhere you look. Business leaders rate customer satisfaction and the quality of their products far higher than their customers do.[37] Students, teachers, athletes, musicians, and professionals of every kind seem to have a hard time separating wishful thinking from hard truth. So do all human beings.

In fact, this tendency to overestimate our gifts and abilities is so ingrained in human nature that the apostle Paul begins a major passage on using our God-given gifts in the service of others with this exhortation: "Do not think of yourself more highly than you ought, but rather think of yourself with sober judgment"[38]

HAPPY TALK

To make matters worse, our sense of God-given potential is often inflated by what I call happy talk.

It's become politically incorrect to tell anyone they're not good at something, even when they stink at it.

The formula for maximized potential is strangely similar to the recipe for a nervous breakdown or a broken home.

From preschool on, many of us have been rewarded with smiley faces and happy stickers no matter what. "You can do it" is always supposed to be the appropriate response.

Even if it's obvious we can't.

After a while, some of us actually start to believe the happy talk, ratcheting up our self-perceived potential to a higher level with each hollow compliment.

It doesn't stop as we grow older. High schools and colleges grapple with rampant grade inflation. Job reviews say "well done" even when the boss isn't too happy.

As a pastor, I get feedback each weekend after a message. If you stood beside me and listened to the comments, you'd think I was one of the great communicators of all time.

But come on. What else can people say? Social convention calls for a compliment. Even if my message was the worst ever, no one's going to say, "Larry, that was a real dog. Better luck next week."

(As an aside, that's why I've learned to put all my stock in second-hand compliments. They're the only ones not tainted by social conventions. When someone tells someone else—not me—that I did well or that something I said or did was particularly helpful, odds are it was. Unless of course they were talking to my mother.)

But the biggest problem with the unquestioned pursuit of potential is that sooner or later it gets in the way of obedience, serving others, and a thing called love.

OBEDIENCE

We've all seen it: A well-schooled Christian decides that being all he or she can be is more important than keeping a promise, fulfilling commitments, or providing for an inconvenient spouse or family member.

So they chuck it all to pursue their own dream.

But Jesus didn't say, "If you love me, you'll fulfill your potential." He said, "If you love me, *you will obey what I command.*"[39]

There's no way around it; obeying the clear commands of Scripture sometimes short-circuits our potential.

When our oldest son, Nathan, was seven years old, he told his mother, "I don't like it when Dad writes; he doesn't play with me."

I'd just started my third book. The previous one had taken only a short period of concentrated effort, since much of it was based on a series of articles I'd previously published.

But in his mind, those weeks felt like years.

The compass of potential said, "Find a way to finish this new book. God is obviously opening doors. You're good at writing. It's a calling."

But the compass of Scripture said, "Be a great dad. Your family is more important than your ministry. Your primary job is to pass the spiritual torch to the next generation."

So I put the book down. Nancy and I decided I wouldn't write another one until our kids were out of high school.

This is that next book.

Now, I'm not trying to force the same decision on anyone else who writes. Each of us has our own path to take. But for Nancy and me, setting aside the potential to write a few more books was an easy choice.

Obedience always trumps potential.

There's no question that my obedience resulted in some God-given talents sitting on the shelf for years. My résumé is far less impressive. My influence is decidedly smaller. The lost time can never be made up.

But I have three kids who love God, love the church their dad serves, and love their dad. It was the right decision. I'd do it again any day.

Obedience always trumps potential.

SERVING OTHERS

The hot pursuit of potential also tends to get in the way of serving others.

Our culture asks, "How big is your entourage? How many on your staff? How large the crowd? How wide the influence?"

Jesus asks, "Who are you serving?"

He once said,

> Whoever wants to become great among you must be your servant, and whoever wants to be first must be your slave—just as the Son of Man did not come to be served, but to serve, and to give his life as a ransom for many."[40]

That's a far cry from realizing our potential.

WHILE POTENTIAL seeks greatness in being all *I* can be, serving others seeks greatness in helping others be all *they* can be.

For John the Baptist, that meant introducing Jesus to the public, then stepping into the background. For Barnabas, it meant letting Paul take center stage. For some of us, it means playing second fiddle with first-fiddle gifts, fulfilling a commitment we wish we'd never made, or dying to a dream while helping someone else achieve theirs.

Serving others will never be easy. The lure of fulfilling our potential will always be enticing. But for those of us who want to experience genuine God-pleasing spirituality, the tough road of servanthood is the way to get there.

A THING CALLED LOVE

It's no news flash that sacrificially loving others is an important part of the Christian life.

But those of us who seek to find fulfillment on the highway called potential will almost always have to leave such service behind at some point.

Sooner or later it just gets in the way.

Years ago, a college president created quite a stir when he resigned his post to become the primary caregiver for his ailing wife (she had advanced Alzheimer's disease). He was praised in many circles, criticized in others. To all the potential-junkies, he was fool. They saw his wife as a lost cause, her fate sealed—while he had so much more still to do.

J. Robertson McQuilkin was in his mid-fifties. As far as college presidents go, he had a lot of years left. But he'd also promised his wife, Muriel, that he'd be there for her, for better or worse.

He decided his higher calling was to care for his wife. He walked away from his prestigious role to spend his days cooking, cleaning, and caring for her needs.

A few years into it, he attended a workshop where the presenting "expert" claimed that there were only two reasons why anyone would keep a family member at home instead of in a nursing facility: economic necessity and guilt.

When McQuilkin challenged her afterward that there might be a third reason, she insisted: No, just two.

"What about love?" he asked.

She replied, "Oh, we put that under guilt."[41]

So much for love.

If the master asks me to serve his family by making sure his guests are well fed, it doesn't matter if I have the gifts to be a virtuoso; I belong in the kitchen, not the concert hall.

———

To a culture enamored with the allure of self-actualization and fully realized potential, love is fine—as long as it doesn't get in the way.

But let it threaten to become a major distraction, an impassable roadblock, or a heavy burden, and it'll be quickly left behind, jettisoned in favor of the far more alluring goal of reaching our fullest potential.

Which is why I'm so leery of this thing I call the Potential Trap. And why I believe trying to become all we can be is often the worst thing we could ever do.

CHAPTER TWENTY

GLASS HOUSE LIVING

Why Accountability Groups Don't Work

EARLY IN MY JOURNEY with God, I heard about something that supposedly had the power to keep me on the straight and narrow even when I wanted to wander off.

It was called an "accountability group."

It apparently had magical powers. All I had to do was find a group of likeminded friends who shared my desire to know God. If we would commit to meet weekly, ask each other tough questions, and pray for one another, we'd stand strong. We'd never fall.

It sounded too good to be true.

It was.

NOW, LET ME be clear that I'm not against accountability partners or groups. They're not a bad thing. Under the right circumstances they can do a lot of good. At times they've helped turbo-charge my own spiritual growth. Other times they've pushed me to keep after things I would have otherwise let slide.

It's just that they're overrated.

Highly overrated.

A CURIOUS ABSENCE

The first thing giving me pause is that I can't find an accountability group anywhere in the Bible.

The Scriptures are strangely silent about something that, from my earliest days as a Christian, I was repeatedly told I needed if I wanted to successfully fight off sin's strongest urges.

That strikes me as odd.

That's not to say the absence of a specific command or biblical example means we should put an end to the practice. It's just to say that this may not be the biblical panacea everyone told me it was. And it's certainly not a mandatory prerequisite for spiritual growth and maturity.

The New Testament does place an emphasis on authentic relationships. It commands openness and honesty. But it's always within the framework of a local church, not a small group of friends agreeing to meet off-line for an *extra* dose of candor and accountability.

KEEPING ON TRACK

There's one thing accountability partners and groups do especially well. They keep us on track, motivating us to keep after a specific task or spiritual discipline long after we would have quit if left on our own.

When I decided to memorize larger chunks of Scripture, I first tried to do it on my own. I'd go great guns for a week or two, then hit a wall. Eventually I'd pick it up again, only to run out of steam before long.

Then one day I discovered that a friend was also into memorizing. We decided to meet each Tuesday afternoon to check up on our progress.

I still hit the same wall, but it no longer stopped me. I wish I could say it was due to a renewed hunger to know God's word. But it wasn't.

It was my fear of The Look.

When Tuesday afternoon came, my friend would ask me to recite my latest set of verses. If I didn't have any, he'd smile, look at me with a knowing gaze, then launch into his verses for the week.

I hated that look. I'd go to great lengths to avoid it. Many Monday nights I stayed up long past getting tired to review old verses and memorize new ones, just to keep from having to see it again.

Glass House Living recognizes that the best way to help a friend overcome an addiction like internet pornography is to have him put his computer in the living room, install a program that records every site he visits, and give his wife unfettered access to it.

This beats hands-down a weekly meeting with a group of friends who struggle with the same issues and who covenant to ask each other if they've looked at anything they shouldn't have lately.

It's too easy to lie to the group. But it's hard to lie to yourself or anyone else when your wife is standing there looking over your shoulder.

It's far easier and more effective to wage the battle against this and many other areas of sin and spiritual weakness by removing the cloak of privacy and replacing it with the bright lights of transparency.

That's why I'm such a big fan of Glass House Living. It puts flesh and bones to the ethereal truth that I'm being watched and that I'll one day be judged. It brings the future into the present.

The value of our accountability partnership was obvious. It consistently spurred me on to do what I otherwise would have put off. It kept me on track even when I wanted to bail out.

TOUGH QUESTIONS—BLATANT LIES

Yet, ironically, the one thing most people think accountability groups do best is what they don't do well at all.

They're not good at preventing sin.

Whether it's a tell-all partner or a small group committed to asking tough questions and keeping each other's feet to the fire, let's-help-each-other-stay-away-from-sin accountability groups seldom work as advertised.

I REMEMBER the first time I joined one. We were a group of college guys wanting to live a life of sexual purity. We all wanted the Spirit to have control. But the hormones raged.

Our solution was to form a sexual purity accountability group. We assumed we'd all live up to a higher standard knowing we had to tell the truth to the rest of the group each week when we met.

The thought of having to come clean was supposed to give us pause before giving in to temptation. It was supposed to lead to higher standards in our dating relationships. It was supposed to keep our thought lives pure, to ward off the temptations of pornography, to give victory over inappropriate self-gratification. It was supposed to...

Well, it was supposed to.

But it didn't.

The problem?

Guys lied. Big, bold-faced lies.

When I first found out I was devastated. The sole purpose of our meetings was truth-telling and accountability. I couldn't understand how a couple of the guys could show up each week, look me in the eye, and keep on lying. Not just once or twice, but week after week, month after month.

But now I understand.

SHAME-BASED SIN

The Achilles' heel of any accountability group designed to restrain sin is our tendency to lie—especially about things that are uncomfortable, embarrassing, or shame-producing.

Let's face it: Some things are easier to confess than others.

In most groups, it's not too hard to admit that we lost it with the wife or the kids, lied about a check being in the mail, or flipped the bird to someone who cut us off on the freeway. People relate. They're quick to voice support. Sometimes they even laugh.

But other failings are not so easy to bring to light—drug or alcohol abuse, sexual addictions, the early flirtations of an emotional affair, the first kiss of the real deal, embezzling to pay the bills.

All these are classic examples of shame-based sin. Bringing any one of them to the light produces a strong sense of embarrassment and shame. So most people keep such failures in the dark, even after promising they wouldn't.

I learned the strong connection between shame and deception the hard way—dealing with families devastated by the evil of sexual molestation.

In each and every case, the perpetrator lied the longest and most vehemently to those he was closest to, to those who most expected the truth.

That made it even more crushing when the truth came out. Family members and close friends felt doubly betrayed. They had seen themselves as being in the same corner as the accused, and they assumed they would be the first to hear the truth.

But that's not how shame works. Since the people who are most in our corner tend to believe in us even when no one else does, we'll often do whatever it takes to keep them there. As the walls cave in, their respect and support may be the only thing we've got left.

So we lie.

Failing to grasp this strong connection between shame-based sin and blatant lies set me up to be betrayed and deeply disillusioned when my friends failed to tell the truth they'd promised to tell.

I hadn't realized that even the most well-intentioned accountability partners will have a hard time telling the truth when the truth is embarrassing or shameful.

A MORE POWERFUL TOOL

I no longer expect too much from the process. When I find myself in a so-called accountable relationship, I recognize that the only thing I can know and control is whether I'm telling the truth. I can never know for sure about others.

There's no magical power in the meeting, no magical power in the questions. Adam lied to God. So did Cain. It shouldn't be too surprising that we lie to each other.

All this is not to say I've given up on the concept of accountability. It just means I no longer look to a small group of friends to provide the bulk of it.

Instead, I've turned to a much more powerful tool. I call it Glass House Living.

Instead of depending on a few close friends to ask tough questions about what I did *last* week, I've increased the number of people who can see what I'm doing *this* week—and see it in real time.

Glass House Living is a personal commitment to two primary things: (1) as much transparency as possible, and (2) an open-door policy.

TRANSPARENCY

Glass House Living is based on the simple observation that anonymity and secrecy breed sin.

When no one else sees or knows what I'm doing, temptation is far more enticing. But if I know I'm being watched, I'll most often do the right thing, even if I don't want to.

That's why we slow down when we see a cop in the rearview mirror. Why a sailor's language cleans up in the presence of Mom. Why the kids never steal a cookie when the whole family is in the kitchen.

It's also the reason that virtually every major airport has a Dirty Dan's nearby. Purveyors of smut know that their clients are more likely to come in for a drink and a lap dance in a town where no one knows them. Put that same establishment a couple of blocks from home, and most of their customers would drive right by.

I do not understand what I do. For what I want to do I do not do, but what I hate I do.... For what I do is not the good I want to do; no, the evil I do not want to do—this I keep on doing.... So I find this law at work: When I want to do good, evil is right there with me. For in my inner being I delight in God's law; but I see another law at work in the members of my body, waging war against the law of my mind and making me a prisoner of the law of sin at work within my members. (Romans 7:15–23)

Unfortunately, our culture's love affair with privacy has elevated it to the status of a divine right. The result is that we now have large islands of secrecy and anonymity where we used to have transparency.

It's supposedly no one's business what I watch or download in the privacy of my home. Child psychologists tell me my children's rooms are off limits. Lawyers tell me I can pay for my kids' college tuition, but I have no right to access their grades or medical records.

The Bible knows no such right to privacy, especially when it's used as a cloak to hide things we'd never do if others were watching. In fact, the Bible promises the opposite, a coming day when everything will be brought to light, scrutinized, and judged.

Glass House Living recognizes that any privacy I may have now is only temporary, that our closets will one day be opened wide. So why not let people go ahead and peek in now?

AN OPEN DOOR

Glass House Living also gives some trusted people permission to barge in without knocking.

Few of us fall apart spiritually overnight. It usually begins with a series of small steps and compromises.

But if my life is a closed book, so private that I reveal what I want to reveal only when I'm comfortable revealing it, these small steps and compromises will mostly remain unknown and unchallenged.

One group, however, almost always notices the first signs of even the slightest step in the wrong direction. It's the people we live and spend the most time with. They might not be able to pinpoint what's wrong, but they intuitively know something is.

Unfortunately, our social conventions don't give these folks permission to speak up early. It's not cool to butt in unless you've been invited in.

Granting a fairly large circle of friends and co-workers the right to barge in and express their unease at the first sign of concern is a powerful way to keep small things from morphing into big things. A candid conversation early on is a lot easier on everyone than a tough intervention after things have gotten out of hand.

> **We give each other permission to barge into our lives and make the danger known before it becomes a problem.**

I've also found that those closest to me not only catch the early signs of spiritual slippage, they also tend to recognize a potentially dangerous situation long before I do. Glass House Living gives them permission to barge in and make the danger known before it becomes a problem.

A group of us have long practiced Glass House Living in terms of our relationships with the opposite sex. We're all married men. We all work with women. So we've given each other permission to step in and squash any working relationship that sends off vibes we don't feel right about.

It doesn't matter how "innocent" the relationship might be. It's over once one of us barges in and gives notice.

These same friends have walked into my office and called me to task about decisions, perceived changes in attitude, and things I've said or done. They've even waded into how I spend my time and my money.

I can't say I've always enjoyed the process or the easy accessibility. At times I've wanted to trade in the glass house for a fortress—one with a moat.

But truth be known, it has saved me a ton of grief.

It has provided an early warning system. It has identified on the front end issues that otherwise would have gone undetected for a long time. It has made it hard for me to hide, pretend, or cover up.

Sometimes they've jumped in too early. At times they've had the facts all wrong. But no matter, because each time they've barged in, they put me back on notice that people are watching. And when I know people are watching, I always live to a higher standard.

I WISH I could say my knowledge that God watches everything is enough to keep me on the straight and narrow. I wish my strong belief in a future day of judgment was enough to scare me away from sin.

But it's not.

Adam's curse is too strong.

For most of us, knowing that an unseen God sees everything and that we face a future day of reckoning proves pretty weak in the face of a tangible and strong present-day temptation.

Even the apostle Paul bemoaned the fact that he had a hard time doing what he knew to be right and avoiding what he knew to be wrong.[42]

Glass House Living undercuts the subtle temptations of secrecy and anonymity. It sheds light into the otherwise dark corners of my life.

And it picks up where our accountability groups drop off by radically widening the circle of people who can see into my life and step in to do something about it.

When people can see in the windows, there's usually no need to ask the tough questions. They already know.

CHAPTER TWENTY-ONE

PRIORITY NUMBER ONE?

Why Putting God First Might Be a Bad Idea

WHEN IT COMES to listing our priorities, everyone seems to know the right answer. It's God first; family second; and after that, anything we choose.

The top of the list is always the same. The order never varies.

Of course that doesn't mean we really live by these priorities. It just means we know the politically correct answer.

But I learned early on in my Christian journey that I was supposed to be different. I was actually expected to *live* by the list.

I was taught to give to God the first part of everything, from time to money.

I was warned about the pitfalls of putting work and career above God and family.

And everywhere I looked, there were reminders of Jesus' command to seek first the kingdom of God. It was plastered on all kinds of Jesus junk, from coffee mugs and posters to key chains and bookmarks.

It was hard to miss.

Frankly, I had no idea what it meant.

WHAT DOES "FIRST" MEAN?

Is being "first" simply a priority of *order*?

Does putting God first mean starting each day with prayer and Bible study? And if that's the case, how much time do I need to spend before I'm free to go on to the next thing? Is there a minimum requirement? Can I rush it on the busy days?

Or is it a priority of *time*?

Does putting God first mean giving him more hours out of my day? That's easy to do as long as I'm a student, a missionary, a pastor, or in some form of full-time ministry. But it's nearly impossible to find more hours if I'm a salesman, a business owner, or the mother of a couple of preschoolers.

Maybe it's a priority of *quality*?

Perhaps putting God first means always giving him the best portion of my time and energy. But isn't my employer paying me to do the same thing? And shouldn't I do my best in everything anyway? Surely God isn't excusing schlocky work elsewhere.

Could it be a priority of *value*?

Could putting God first mean that whenever I'm faced with options, God and his agenda should always be the first choice? But again, how far does that go? Am I supposed to be at the church every time the doors open? Can I skip a prayer meeting to hang with my friends? Can I read a novel when there's a Bible on the nightstand?

I don't think I'm alone in asking these questions. For many of us, the idea of making God our number one priority is a nebulous concept. We can make it incorporate all the above or exclude any of the above, depending on the situation or circumstances we're in—which conveniently means that whatever we do, we can probably find a way to still claim we're putting God first.

———

After years of muddling along trying to make God my first priority but never being quite sure what it meant, I finally gave up.

> I stopped putting God first. I put him in the middle.

I stopped putting God first.

I put him in the middle.

Imagine a circle or a wheel with a hub and spokes. Now put God in the center hub. Each of the spokes represents an area or activity of life. It might be work, family, church, friends, interaction with your kids or spouse, mowing the lawn, or taking a nap.

Whatever it is, now imagine doing it for God.

That's the idea behind these words from the apostle Paul:

> Whatever you do, whether in word or deed, do it all in the name of the Lord Jesus, giving thanks to God the Father through him.[43]

The key to this passage is found in the command to do everything "*in the name of the Lord Jesus.*"

IN JESUS' NAME?

So what does it mean to do something "in Jesus' name"? The phrase gets thrown around a lot in Christian circles. But I'm afraid it's one of those things we say without having much of an idea what it really means.

As a new Christian I noticed that almost everyone tacked it on at the end of their prayers. When I asked why, I was told it was because Jesus had promised to answer our prayers and requests as long as they were asked "in his name."

So I tacked it on, not quite sure if it was a magical phrase that forced God to give me what I asked for—sort of like a genie obligated to grant the wish of anyone who knows the secret incantation—or just the "send" button that propelled my prayers through the heavens.

To this day it still feels strange and incomplete when I hear someone end a prayer without some version of the "in his name" phrase.

But the apostle Paul obviously didn't have a magical phrase in mind when he challenged us to do everything in the name of Jesus. He wasn't asking us to go through the day constantly muttering "in Jesus' name" as if suffering from a rare form of spiritual Tourette's syndrome.

No, he had something else in mind. He was challenging us to bring God into everything we do, to begin seeing every action and event as an opportunity to represent God well.

When a lawyer uses the power of attorney to represent a client, he's acting in the name and best interest of his client. When an emissary travels to a distant land, he acts and speaks in the name of the king.

When we approach every task and life situation as an opportunity to further God's agenda, advance his kingdom or make him look good, we're doing whatever we do "in his name." In effect, we've put him in the center.

WHAT ABOUT "SEEK YE FIRST"?

You may be thinking, "But didn't Jesus say to seek God first?"

No. He didn't.

I don't mean to be picky. But Jesus didn't suggest that we put God first, family second, and so on. The quote in question comes from the Sermon on the Mount. It comes at the end of a discourse on the folly of worrying about our earthly provisions. Jesus says,

> But seek first his kingdom and his righteousness, and all
> these things will be given to you as well. Therefore do not
> worry about tomorrow, for tomorrow will worry about
> itself. Each day has enough trouble of its own.[44]

The context and the conclusion ("Therefore do not worry")
makes it clear Jesus wasn't asking to be first on some priority list.
He was telling us to stop worrying about earthly concerns and to
start laying up heavenly treasures.

And that's a very different thing than putting God first in a
laundry list of priorities.

AM I DONE YET?

One of the problems with trying to make God the first priority on
a hierarchical list is that we're never really done with God.

Frankly, if I was really putting God first, family second, work
third, and so on, I'd never show up for work.

There will always be more things to pray about. More of the
Bible to read. More people to care for. And if I should ever finish
all the things on my God list, I've got a family with needs that
would easily suck up the rest of the day. We've never yet gotten in
enough quality time. I've never come close to completing my
honey-do list.

IS GOD IN THE BOX?

But the biggest problem with putting God first on a priority checklist is that it breaks life into two boxes: the spiritual box and the
secular box.

The spiritual box contains all the God stuff—church, ministry, Bible studies, service projects, and maybe family and Christian friends.

The secular box contains everything else.

WHEN WE SEE GOD as the first priority on a list rather than the center of everything we do, we have a strong tendency to assume that taking care of the things in the God box equals putting God first.

Even worse, there's also a strong tendency to assume that God doesn't have much to do with the stuff in the secular box.

That's why so many Christians who would never tell a lie at church have no problem stretching the truth on a sales call. Why some of us have no qualms about telling a dirty joke in the cubicle that we'd never tell in the vestibule.

The spiritual/secular dichotomy is a devilish worldview. I mean that literally. If I was the enemy, I couldn't think of a better bargain. It gives God his dues in one area in exchange for keeping him out of everything else.

TAKING GOD off the top of my priority list and putting him in the center of my life helped me break the last vestiges of spiritual/secular dichotomy in my own life. It's helped me see *all* of life as spiritual—everything I do as part of my larger assignment from God.

When I was working my way through college, I didn't yet understand this principle. I still saw God as my first priority, and I still divided my daily schedule into two categories, spiritual and secular.

During the day, I took a few Bible classes at a local Christian college. At night, I stocked shelves for a local grocery store. As I stocked those shelves, I often dreamed of the day when I would be finished with school and could spend my time in full-time ministry.

It never dawned on me that I was already in full-time Christian ministry.

I saw my early morning Bible classes, personal prayer, and quiet time with God as my highest priority (the God box). I saw stocking shelves at Alpha Beta Market as a much lower priority (the secular box).

This blinded me to the fact that I was actually in the middle of an amazing short-term special assignment. God had entrusted me with a front-line opportunity to infiltrate a godless work environment. As far as I knew, I was the only Christian on the entire crew.

What an opportunity.

But I missed much of it. I saw it as just part of the secular box, something to endure on my way to a brighter day when I could spend more time in the God box. It never occurred to me that I was representing God just as much when stocking those shelves as I would be when standing up to deliver a sermon.

Would it have made a big difference if I'd recognized the truth?

I'm convinced it would have—and that it always will make a difference when we take God off the top of some list and put him in the middle of our lives where he belongs.

A FINAL WORD

Keeping It Simple

A STRANGE THING HAPPENS with most regulated professions. Over the years the bar to entry is slowly raised by those who are already in.

The excuse is always the same: A desire to keep the unqualified out and to protect the reputation of the profession.

The result is a greater sense of exclusivity and often a set of rules and regulations that would keep the people raising the bar from getting in themselves if they had to start over.

You can see the same thing happen with families who flee the suburbs or city for a more pristine rural setting. They're all for growth and easy building codes when moving in. But once enough of their old neighbors start to follow, it's not long until a slow-growth or no-growth initiative shows up on the ballot.

God's people are no different. We've always had a tendency to try raising the bar to entry—*after* we've gotten in.

We're still doing it.

The simplicity of knowing God through Jesus Christ and the accessibility of genuine spirituality get obscured by the thick fog of traditions, well-intentioned extra fences, and our assumption that whatever's good for us would also be great for everybody else.

Whenever the bar gets raised higher than the actual standard set by Jesus and the Bible, the result is a lot of Christians who see themselves as saved yet incapable of ever experiencing a spirituality that genuinely pleases God.

That's a shame, because historically whenever God shows up—whether in the days of the Old Testament prophets, during the ministry of Jesus Christ, or in a modern day revival—the people he calls, uses, and blesses seldom fit the conventional profile of spirituality.

More often than not, they've been culled from ranks of common folks, people like you and me long ago written off by the spiritually elite as lacking the pedigree, education, dedication, or prerequisites for being known and used by God.

But God hasn't seemed to notice or care all that much what they think. He shows up, recruits the humble, broken, and pedestrian, and gives us a path we can follow and a power we can access.

He's the ultimate come-as-you-are God.

Sadly, most non-Christians don't know it and many Christians no longer seem to believe it.

A SACRED CURTAIN once separated God from his people. Only the high priest could come in, and then only once a year. But when Jesus died for us, God himself tore the curtain in two, symbolizing a new day of access.

For some reason, we keep sewing it back together, thinking we're helping God out or protecting his reputation.

He needs neither.

———

I ONCE THOUGHT spirituality at its highest levels was out of reach, reserved for those who were a lot smarter, more dedicated, and wired the right way.

I realize now it wasn't God who sent that message. It wasn't God who raised the bar beyond my reach.

Without apology, I've attempted in this book to point us back to a form of spirituality that can be accessed by anyone willing to let Jesus come in and take over. I've tried to rip down our re-sewn curtains and lower the bar back to the place where God set it.

If I've been unsuccessful at any point, please forgive me. I've done my best. But on this side of heaven, there will always be blind spots, always some static on the line.

Fortunately, you can always find the right measurements and recalibrations within the pages of the Scripture.

Like here…in the words of the prophet Micah:

> With what shall I come before the LORD and bow down before the exalted God? Shall I come before him with burnt offerings, with calves a year old? Will the LORD be pleased with thousands of rams, with ten thousand rivers of oil? Shall I offer my firstborn for my transgression, the fruit of my body for the sin of my soul? He has showed you, O man, what is good. And what does the LORD require of you? To act justly and to love mercy and to walk humbly with your God.[45]

Blessings on your journey,
Larry Osborne

ACKNOWLEDGMENTS

I WANT TO especially thank Doug Gabbert and Thomas Womack for your belief in me and the importance of getting this message out. Without your encouragement and support, these thoughts and principles would have likely remained forever buried in my soul.

I also want to thank Charlie Bradshaw, Chris Brown and Paul Savona. No man could have better colaborers in the kingdom. Your hard work and powerful gifts have allowed me to focus on writing this book and have taught me many of the lessons contained within. I love being called your friend.

To the Elder Board of North Coast Church, a special thanks for giving me the freedom to serve the kingdom both near and far. Your godly wisdom has always served me well.

To the entire staff and congregation of North Coast Church, thank you for giving me the incredible privilege of being one of your pastors. You've often served as the testing ground for the practicality and real-world application of many of the principles in this book. As we've journeyed together over the decades, we've learned together what it means to truly know God and please him in a way that genuinely works for all of us. I'm proud of you and your walk with God.

Finally…Nancy and Nathan, I don't know how to thank you for the confidence you gave me as you read and critiqued all the early drafts. I think every writer writes with a nagging doubt as to whether or not the page actually says what he wants it to say. I always knew I could trust your judgment and honesty. You encouraged the good stuff and kindly let me know whenever an idea, principle, or chapter wasn't yet ready for prime time. Thank you for making this book so much better and clearer. The good stuff bears your fingerprints. The not-so-good bears mine.

NOTES

1. See Matthew 3:17
2. Matthew 3:7
3. Luke 7:31–35
4. Philippians 3:12–15
5. 2 Peter 2:1–4
6. Hebrews 10:24–25
7. Romans 1:18–32
8. Proverbs 4:18–19
9. Romans 8:9
10. Philippians 2:12–13
11. Isaiah 30:1–3
12. Numbers 33:52
13. 1 Kings 22:43; 2 Kings 12:2–3; 2 Kings 14:3–4; 2 Kings 15:3–4; see also 1 Kings 15:11,14
14. 1 Kings 15:14
15. Daniel 3:16–17
16. Daniel 3:18
17. Luke 17:3–4
18. Revelation 2:4–5
19. Revelation 2:5